In a Persian Kitchen

FAVORITE RECIPES FROM THE NEAR EAST

by Maideh Mazda

Illustrations by M. Kuwata

TUTTLE PUBLISHING
Boston · Rutland, Vermont · Tokyo

In a Persian Kitchen

For those who look upon cooking as a creative art and a constant challenge, discovering the exquisite cuisine of the Near East is an exciting experience indeed. Over centuries of lavish and exotic living and widespread travel, the Persians, Azerbaijanis, and other peoples of the Near East have developed the many rich and varied recipes for which they are justly famous.

This book now makes it possible for the modern housewife to prepare a large variety of authentic Near Eastern delicacies economically and easily. Included are clear and concise instructions for preparing yogurt, appetizers, soups, stuffed vegetables and fruits, pilâfs, egg casserole dishes, meat and fowl dishes, salads, and desserts. Translating "a pinch of this" and "a pinch of that" into exact measurements familiar to the modern housewife, Maideh Mazda successfully teaches the delicate combination of flavors, characteristic of genuine Near Eastern dishes. Among the exotic recipes are those combining rice with saffron, beef with fresh peaches, chicken with pomegranate syrup, meat stuffed in grape leaves, Baklava with rose water, and many more.

Maideh Mazda, now married to an American and living in America, was born in Persia and while still a little girl was initiated into the mysteries of Persian cuisine. She spent two years compiling the recipes in the book, having cooked and served each dish many times, with the two aims of authenticity and ease of preparation constantly in mind. There will be few gourmets and creative cooks to deny that she has been remarkably successful.

First published in Japan by Tuttle Publishing, an imprint of Periplus Editions (HK) Ltd., with editorial offices at 153 Milk Street, Boston, Massachusetts 02109.

Library of Congress Catalog Card Number: 60006926

ISBN: 0-8048-1619-0

Distributed by:

North America
Tuttle Publishing
Distribution Center
Airport Industrial Park
364 Innovation Drive
North Clarendon, VT 05759-9436
Tel: (802) 773-8930
Fax: (802) 773-6993
Email: info@tuttlepublishing.com
Web site: www.tuttlepublishing.com

Japan
Tuttle Publishing
Yaekari Building, 3rd Floor
5-4-12 Ōsaki, Shinagawa-ku, Tokyo
Japan 141-0032
Tel: (03) 5437-0171
Fax: (03) 5437-0755
Email: tuttle-sales@gol.com

Asia Pacific
Berkeley Books Pte Ltd
130 Joo Seng Road
#06-01/03 Olivine Building
Singapore 368357
Tel: (65) 6280-3320
Fax: (65) 6280-6290
Email: inquiries@periplus.com.sg

Indonesia
PT Java Books Indonesia
JI. Kelapa Gading Kirana
Blok A14 No. 17
Jakarta 14240 Indonesia
Email: cs@javabooks.co.id

08 07 06 05 04   12 11 10 9 8

Printed in the United States of America

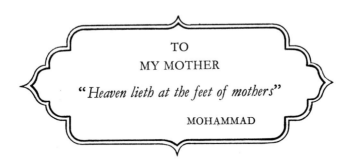

TO
MY MOTHER

"Heaven lieth at the feet of mothers"

MOHAMMAD

Contents

Acknowledgments

This book had its beginning several years ago when two of my very dear college friends, Joanie Rush and Martin Stow, persuaded me to write down the recipes for the many Persian dishes I had cooked for them. Joanie, a very practical American housewife, was anxious to find short cuts for the more elaborate recipes. She wanted my recipes to be economical, easy to prepare, and still retain their exotic qualities. On the other hand, Martin, a gourmet in his own right, insisted that the recipes be kept as authentic as possible. Indeed without this sort of balance which my two friends provided I would have been unable to make these recipes authentic and yet practical.

While writing a first book, the assistance and encouragement of friends are most welcome. Among my friends who have graciously sampled my recipes, I would like to express my appreciation to Marianne Mandel for her culinary advice and to Frank Dines, a connoisseur of foreign foods and an excellent artist, for his kind advice concerning the design and illustrations of the book. Thanks are also due Dr. and Mrs. H. A. Esfandiary, who generously made available a variety of reproductions of Persian art work from which many of the designs were taken.

In writing this book I was anxious to make the accompanying stories colorful and interesting. Since English is not my native language, there were times when I could not express myself perfectly, and I would like to thank my husband, Charles Magee, for his enthusiasm, understanding, and excellent editing.

Finally I want to thank my mother, who has been so patient in testing every recipe with me and who has advised and guided me step by step. I would also like to thank Maryam Mehran and my many friends, Persian and American, for encouraging me and for being gracious guests while I tried out every recipe on them.

I have enjoyed many delightful hours while perfecting these recipes. Now the finished product is yours. Try these dishes, and I do hope that you enjoy them. As we say in Persian, "*Nushe Janetan Bashad,*" or *bon appétit.*

MAIDEH MAZDA

Introduction

As long as I can remember I have always been fond of good food and have always taken an interest in cooking. I believe that my interest in cooking began when I was a little girl and lived with my grandmother in Baku, Russia. Grandmother, who was an extraordinary woman for her time, was a tall, strong, and very handsome lady. In her deep-set black eyes one could see the kindness, generosity, and hospitality for which the Persians have always been famous.

Grandmother was Persian. She was born in Tabriz, Azerbaijan. She came from an old Persian family and her ancestors had lived in Persia for generations. She came to Baku to stay with my mother when we children were born and she remained there.

Grandmother was an extremely active person. She loved people and believed in serving them in any way she could. From her father she learned the art of medicine and practiced it in Baku. She loved company and entertained at any hour of the day. Our house was always full of people, and we had company for lunch, tea, and dinner, and often guests stayed on for weeks or months.

I was brought up in a rather large family. I had one sister and two brothers, but, as in many Persian families, several cousins, uncles, and aunts also lived with us. Some one of us was always entertaining a guest. In addition, Baku attracted Persian merchants, tourists, and students who were on their way to Europe to study. Since we were one of the few Persian families living there, we were always entertaining and taking care of our fellow Persians.

Grandmother, of course, had a hand in bringing up the family and taking care of the guests in customary Persian fashion. She supervised the meals and saw to it that everything was prepared in the most gracious way. She always taught us to be polite and generous. She quoted well-known proverbs and poetry and taught us the hospitality for which her ancestors were famous.

When Grandmother reminded us of our duties to our guests, she often quoted a famous Persian saying: *Mehmân Hediyeh Khodâst*, which means, "A guest is God's gift." Perhaps it is because of such proverbs that the Persian housewives have taken pride in preserving their family recipes. When a guest, expected or not, enters a Persian home, he is treated with the utmost politeness and generosity. No matter how modest a family's income may be, its members have learned from their ancestors to offer their guests the best food and lodging. A modern Persian is really not much different from his ancestors, who could afford to live in lavish palaces and have many servants. Although today in Persia, as in most countries, lavish entertaining is limited, the Persian housewife still understands the art of cooking. Most Persian housewives have servants and cooks, but they themselves still take pride in insuring that their tables have the most palatable dishes.

Grandmother was my idol. I used to follow her as she went

about the house, watched her with curiosity, and ate every meal she prepared. I believe that I was her favorite and was spoiled by her as any grandchild would have been. Although I was very young and still had an undeveloped palate, I could still appreciate her exotic meals. I can well remember once going to Moscow with my mother. We were visiting friends and took our meals, of course, at their home. I remember that I ate very little and when we returned home, I ran to Grandmother and asked her to prepare some of her famous *polo* (*piláf*). She did, and upon my request, let me sit on our beautiful Persian carpet and enjoy my dinner in the traditional manner.

Although my family resided in Baku for many years, our ways of living, our customs and habits were all Persian. Grandmother and my parents saw to it that we children were brought up according to strict Persian tradition. My father hired tutors to teach us Persian and the principles of the Moslem religion. When my family finally left Russia and returned to Persia, we children were thoroughly familiar with the habits and customs of our native land.

I shall never forget the hospitality of my father's friends on the day of our arrival in Persia. Our ship landed in Bandar Pahlavi, on the Caspian Sea. Friends came to greet us at the pier and took us to their home. It was a beautiful Persian home decorated with Persian rugs and miniatures and lovely family treasures. In those days I remember that the harem system still existed in Iran, and the women and men guests were entertained in different rooms of the house. Naturally my mother and I were escorted to the women's section where the hostess received us, according to ancient Persian tradition, by kissing us on both cheeks.

Later, as we were sitting on soft cushions on the floor, the maid of the house, a girl of sixteen, entered with an ewer, basin, and white towel in her hands. She gracefully bowed before my mother and proceeded to pour water so that Mother could wash her hands. Then she repeated her gentle bow and helped me wash my hands. Her manner and the costume she wore seemed strange to me. In Baku we had no Persian servants, and I had never before seen this traditional costume worn by them.

Kobrâ, the sixteen-year-old maid, was a tall and beautiful girl. She wore long, tight black trousers with ballerina tutu of bright yellow. Her long white blouse was of light muslin and extended over her hips. And over her straight black hair she wore a white kerchief which was pinned under her chin. I shall always remember Kobrâ's big, black almond-shaped eyes which were painted with black *sormeh* (the old-fashioned eyebrow pencil). I was impressed with Kobrâ's costume, and asked my mother whether I could wear one like it. In later years, I learned that these costumes were designed originally by one of the Persian kings who had traveled to Europe and was struck by the ballet dancers there.

After the handwashing ceremony, two servants, similarly attired, entered, bowed before us, and offered us tea. Shortly afterward, these servants spread a white tablecloth over a blue Persian rug and set the "table" for lunch. In those days it was customary to eat lunch on the floor, and I liked this custom very much. The lunch was served in the same traditional way that I had seen my grandmother serve it many times. On a large copper platter the servants brought in various types of *khoreshes* (sauces), *chelo* (cooked rice), *polos* (pilâfs), Nâne Lavâsh (thin

Persian bread), *mâst* (yogurt), Mâhi Dudi (smoked fish), and many other delicacies.

I was very impressed by my fatherland, and quickly fell under the spell of its colorful history. As I grew older I learned that it was through the lavish and exotic living of the former Persian kings, their travel and conquering of many lands and their taste for exquisite food, that the Persians through years had developed the art of delicate cooking. For generations Persians have considered cooking and eating an art, and although they have been forced to discard some of the old traditions, they still preserve their appreciation for delicately flavored food.

The proper use of herbs and spices is an art, and I believe that the Persian housewife through years of patient cooking has captured this art. As I watched my mother create various dishes, I learned that in this land of exquisite miniatures and poetry, the culinary art is handled in an equally artistic manner. Like a Persian poet who takes hours to create his romantic poetry, so does the Persian housewife spend hours in creating dishes for daily consumption.

When I left my fatherland to continue my studies in the United States I realized that I would be leaving behind all the old traditions and would have to develop a new mode of living. Little did I know when I left Persia that someday with the help of modern culinary equipment I would be able to create in a modern American kitchen the same delicacies that my grandmother had in her home.

While I was studying in America, my fellow Persians and my American friends who were interested in Persian culture encouraged me to compile this book and put down on paper the exotic, traditional family recipes. My cooking interest in this country began with my homesick countrymen. I shall never forget the first meal I cooked for these Persian friends when I was a student in New York. It was indeed an accomplishment, for although I had cooked a few meals at home I had never before cooked for a large group of hungry students. Lack of experience and lack of the proper equipment and ingredients were against me. But remembering my grandmother's training and her wise words that "A guest is God's gift," I was able to prepare the traditional Chelo Khoresh (rice with sauce) that the students longed for.

As the years passed, my American friends encouraged me more and more in my cooking and enjoyed the unusual dishes which I prepared for them. Along with appreciation of Persian dishes came the usual requests for recipes. I had of course learned to cook the old-fashioned way. I had seen Grandmother, and, later, Mother, cook without measuring the ingredients. It was always a pinch of this or a dash of that, and when I started to cook I carried on this tradition. By looking I knew whether a certain amount was enough and by tasting, I could tell whether a certain dish had the right spicing. However, I soon realized that an American housewife uses the measuring cup and spoon and that she has to know the precise amount of each ingredient which she uses in her cooking. And, finally, I discovered that the element of time is most important in every American kitchen.

Such were the experiences that led me to compile this book. It has taken me almost two years to test all the recipes in this book. I have cooked every dish and have served it to various American friends. I have tried to make the spicing and ingre-

dients as authentic as possible and yet have tried to use a method that would be economical and easy for any American housewife to follow.

Persian dishes in general are very economical, especially in the types of meat used. The spicing and the other unusual ingredients are used in preparing various sauces which are served with rice. This makes the sauce rich and gives it its delicate flavor. Persians are the only people in the Middle East who know how to combine meat with fresh fruit and dried fruit. Through tradition and necessity they have learned to utilize every available ingredient which their country provides.

In this book I have tried to give you many of the exotic recipes for which the Persians are justifiably famous. You will find recipes for a combination of rice with saffron, beef with fresh peaches, chicken with pomegranate syrup, soup made from dried fruit, meat stuffed in grape leaves, Bâglâva with rose water, and many more. Most of these recipes are common Persian dishes, but there are quite a few which have heretofore been kept as family secrets.

At first glance some of these recipes might seem a little complicated or time-consuming. But in fact almost all of them may be prepared a day in advance and kept in the icebox. Most sauces, for example, taste better when they have been cooked for a long time and kept overnight. These are dishes which can be prepared at leisure, need little attention, and don't spoil when kept over a low fire for several hours.

The preparation of *polo* (pilâf) at first might seem very complicated, but once you make it you will realize that it is a very easy dish to prepare. And when you know how to prepare this basic pilâf, you will realize that the rest of the rice dishes are prepared more or less the same way with slight variations.

Most of the ingredients listed in this book can be purchased in any modern grocery. There are only a few ingredients which are not available in regular stores, and these can be purchased in most Greek or Armenian groceries.

Most of these dishes contain one special and useful quality: they can easily be expanded when unexpected guests drop in. In Persia it is customary for the man of the house to bring home guests without warning his wife. The Persian housewife has solved this problem in many different ways, as I have explained herein.

Yogurt

Mast

Yogurt

Mâst, known in America as yogurt, is used extensively in Persia and all the Middle Eastern and Balkan countries. Many scientists of today attribute the stamina and longevity of the Middle Eastern and Balkan people to mâst. These people are practically immune to ulcers and other stomach ailments. Yet they are among the poorest people in the world and their daily food lacks the vitamins necessary for good health. Yogurt is considered the panacea for human ills, and the Persians' long life is attributed to it.

Mâst, which is now becoming more popular in the Western world, has been known to the Middle Easterners for centuries by different names. The most popular name for mâst is yogurt. In the Balkan countries, Turkey, and in the West you can buy mâst under the name of yogurt. In North Africa and in the Arabic-speaking countries it is known as *leban*. Armenians call it *madzoon*, and the Mongols for centuries have called it *koumis*. It is said that Genghis Khan lived on it during his long marches through Mongolia and the Persian Empire when he couldn't obtain other food.

In Iran, yogurt is the food of the rich as well as the poor. Walking down the avenue at lunch hour in Tehran, you will see the mason, the cobbler, the carpenter, the storekeeper, all using yogurt as their daily food. If you go into a restaurant, you will find yogurt served there in many forms.

A Persian housewife whose ancestors have had this "health food" for generations finds many uses for it. She serves yogurt with meals, makes very delicious warm or cold soup with it, or serves it as a dessert.

For generations the Persians have served yogurt as a soft drink in summer. They dilute it with water, add a pinch of salt, and call it *abdug*. The Iranian housewife keeps abdug on hand and serves it to her family and guests on hot summer days. This drink has served as a perfect substitute for "salt tablets."

In Tehran and other cities of Iran vendors who sell abdug on street corners are familiar sights. Very often they advertise their products with a poem or two from Omar Khayyam and replace Omar's "jug of wine" with a "jug of abdug."

Yogurt may be served with diced cucumbers, green onions, chopped fresh dill, and a pinch of salt and pepper as a salad dish. Quite often yogurt is used for marinating meat. It not only makes the meat tender, but gives the meat a very delicate flavor. As a dessert or as a "pick up" between meals, yogurt can be served with sugar, fresh fruits, canned fruits, preserves, or honey.

Finally, yogurt is recommended by many doctors and housewives for all sorts of ailments. If you have a sunburn, a Persian housewife will tell you to use some yogurt as an ointment. She would also advise her daughter to use yogurt for facials to keep her eternal Oriental youth and beauty.

How to Prepare Yogurt

1 *qt. milk*
2–3 *tbsp. yogurt*

Boil the milk until it is almost ready to spill over the top of the pan. Let cool to a point that, when touched with a finger, it will sting slightly. Take 2–3 tablespoons full of yogurt, put it in a cup and dissolve it with some of the warm milk. (Commercial yogurt can be bought in most stores and may be used as a starter. After having made your own yogurt keep some handy to use as a starter.) When thoroughly dissolved, pour it into the warm milk. Mix well, and then pour the milk into glasses or crockery. Cover with waxed paper. If you have used a crockery bowl, put a plate on top of the bowl and cover it with 3 or 4 dishtowels (top and sides) to keep it at an even temperature. Let it stand overnight in the kitchen away from drafts. It takes 7 to 8 hours to thicken. When ready, yogurt should have the consistency of a custard. Remove covers and store yogurt in refrigerator. Yogurt will keep about a week, but it is suggested that it be made every couple of days in order to retain its fresh taste.

If thicker consistency is desired, add a pint of table cream to milk before boiling. It will give a much richer flavor. For a more solid form put the yogurt in a cheese cloth and hang, letting the water from the yogurt drip for 25–30 minutes. When ready yogurt should have the consistency of cottage cheese.

Appetizers

Panir

Goat's Cheese

Panir, or goat's cheese, is an extremely delicious cheese which the Persians habitually eat. If you walk down the avenue in Tehran during lunch hour, you will find the mason, the cobbler, the storekeeper—everybody—eating *nân va panir*, or bread and cheese. Persians bake two kinds of bread, called Nâne Lavâsh and Nâne Sangak. Nâne Lavâsh is very thin bread which is crisp and can be kept for days. Nâne Sangak, which is baked on hot pebbles, should be eaten fresh and warm.

Very often Persians eat nân va panir with either fresh mint or fresh tarragon. In summer, when grapes are abundant, they eat nân va panir with grapes. Panir may be bought in Greek or Armenian stores, where it is called *fetâ*. I have served panir many times as an appetizer with cocktails and have found that my American friends are very fond of it. Try serving panir with crackers or melba toast and you will be a very popular host.

"The first duty of a host is cheerfulness."
ARAB WISDOM

Mast va Khiar

Yogurt with Cucumbers

1 1/2 *cups yogurt*
1 *cucumber*
1 *tbsp. fresh dill* or 1 *tsp. dill weed*
salt and pepper

Put the yogurt in a bowl. Peel and chop the cucumber finely and add it to the yogurt. Add finely chopped dill and salt and pepper to taste and mix well. Let this stay in the frigidaire for 1/2 hour before serving. Mâst va Khiâr may be served as an appetizer or as a substitute for salad. *Makes 3–4 servings.*

Borani Bademjan

Eggplant Hors d'oeuvre

2 *eggplants*
2 *tbsp. salt*
6 *tbsp. shortening*

2 *cloves garlic (chopped)*
1 *cup yogurt*
1 *clove garlic (chopped)*

Cut the eggplants in half (lengthwise), then slice crosswise in 1/2" slices. Wash and salt the eggplants. Set them aside for about 20 minutes. Wash the salt off the eggplants and dry them

 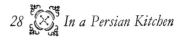

with paper towel. Melt shortening in a skillet and sauté the eggplants and chopped garlic. As you sauté the eggplants, put them on a paper towel to absorb the grease. Let cool. Spread 2 to 3 tablespoons yogurt at the bottom of a dish and arrange the eggplants over it. Add some chopped garlic. Repeat this and top the eggplants with yogurt. Keep in the refrigerator until ready to serve. It is served cold.

Makes 6–7 servings as an hors d'oeuvre.

Borani Esfanaj

Spinach Hors d'oeuvre

1 *lb. spinach*	1/2 *tsp. salt*
1 *cup water*	1/2 *tsp. cinnamon*
1 *medium onion (chopped)*	1/2 *tsp. pepper*
4 *tbsp. butter*	1–2 *cloves garlic (chopped)*
1 *cup yogurt*	

Clean, wash, and chop the spinach. Boil the spinach in water for 10 minutes. Sauté the onions in butter. When the onions are half done, squeeze the water from the spinach and add it to the onions and sauté a few more minutes. Add the spinach and onions to the yogurt, add the seasoning, mix well, let cool, and serve it cold. *Makes 3–4 servings.*

Borani Chogondar

Beet Hors d'oeuvre

1 can sliced beets
4 tbsp. yogurt
1 tbsp. dried mint

Drain water from the beets. Put two tablespoons of yogurt in a dish. Arrange beets in the dish and top it with yogurt. Let it remain in the refrigerator until time to serve. When ready to serve, take the mint and rub it in the palm of your hands and sprinkle it over the beets. *Makes 3–4 servings.*

Borani Garch

Mushroom Hors d'oeuvre

1 lb. fresh mushrooms
1 large onion (chopped)
3 tbsp. butter
1/4 tsp. salt

dash of pepper
3/4 cup yogurt
1/2 tsp. dry mint

Wash, clean, and chop the mushrooms. Sauté the mushrooms and the onions in the butter until golden. Remove and let cool. Add salt and pepper and yogurt and mix. Decorate this with

dry mint and serve it cold. This hors d'oeuvre may be served on toast or crackers.   *Makes 3–4 servings.*

Nazkhatun

Eggplant Caviar

2 *medium eggplants*   1/4 *tsp. cinnamon*
1/2 *cup chopped parsley*   2 *tbsp. vinegar*
2 *cloves garlic*   1 *tbsp. lemon juice*
1 *tsp. salt*   1 *tbsp. dry mint*
1/2 *tsp. pepper*

Wash and bake the eggplants in 350° oven for 1 hour or until done. When done, remove the skin and chop the eggplants. Add chopped parsley and mix well. Squeeze garlic into the eggplant mixture, add the seasoning and vinegar, and mix well. Let stay for a few hours.   *Makes 5–6 servings.*

"Shall I tell you the very worst amongst you? Those who eat alone, and whip the slaves, and give to nobody."
MOHAMMAD

Soups

Ash, which in Persian means soup, is a very popular meal among the Persians. In the old days the Persians were famous for the varieties of ash which they could prepare. There are many stories connected with the preparation of ash and the origin of this dish.

The Persian word for "cook" is *ash-paz*, literally "maker of the soup." The word "kitchen" in Persian is *ash-paz-khâneh*, that is "the house of the cook." This should indicate the importance of the word ash and the role that soup used to play in the lives of ancient Persians.

Ash is basically a very simple dish. The varieties of ash depend on geographic location and the available ingredients. It can be a very simple meal, prepared inexpensively, or it can be a rich meal if one knows how to spice it properly. Persians again use their own original spicing for this basically simple meal, but with a touch of true artistry they create a meal as simple yet as exotic as the poetry of Omar Khayyam and as colorful and rich as the miniatures of Behzad.

In this book, unfortunately, I am not doing justice to the many varieties of ash. I am listing only the ones which are easy to prepare and can be prepared with ingredients readily available.

Ashe Anar

Pomegranate Soup

I always yearn for a certain type of food in a certain month. When the month of October rolls around, I always think of pomegranates. When I look at a pomegranate in a shop it reminds me of long cold winter nights in Tehran where my family used to sit around *korsi** and eat fresh pomegranates which had been prepared by our servant Ozrâ and served with salt or sugar.

Pomegranate is an extremely delicate fruit and rarely recognized in America. Many of my friends have asked me to describe to them a pomegranate. While very delicious and juicy pomegranates are grown in California, unfortunately very few people in this country know how to eat them. In Persia pomegranate is a very popular fruit, and when in season Persian people find many uses for it. In Persia we not only eat this fruit just as it is, but also use it in soups, sauces, desserts, and we drink the juice by squeezing the fruit and then making a hole in the thick skin and sucking it. And, finally, we use the skin for dyeing material and yarns for rugs.

* A low table, about the size of a large coffee table, under which is placed a round charcoal burner. The table is covered with quilts in order to retain the heat. This is a common method of heating Persian homes in winter.

Pomegranate soup is one of the most popular winter soups. When pomegranates are in season, the Persian housewife wouldn't hesitate to serve this soup to her family several times a month. Pomegranate soup is a very delicately flavored soup, and the finished product has a beautiful pink color. This soup can be kept for several days, its flavor improving each day.

Pomegranate Soup

1/2 *lb. ground beef*
1 *small onion (grated)*
1/4 *tsp. cinnamon*
1/4 *tsp. pepper*
1/4 *tsp. salt*
8 *cups water*
2 *tsp. salt*
1/2 *cup rice*
1 *cup spinach (chopped)*
1 *cup parsley (chopped)*
1/2 *cup green onions (chopped)*

1 1/2 *cups pomegranate seeds or* 1
cup pomegranate juice
1/3 *cup sugar*
1 *tbsp. lime juice (optional)*

SPICING OF SOUP

1 *tbsp. dried mint*
1/4 *tsp. cinnamon*
1/4 *tsp. pepper*

Put the meat in a bowl. Add grated onions and seasoning and mix well. Make meat balls the size of walnuts. Put water in a 3-quart pot. Add salt and rice and let cook for 15 minutes. Add vegetables and let cook for another 15 minutes. Cut fresh pomegranate and take out the seeds to make about 1 1/2 cups. Add meat balls, pomegranate seeds, and sugar to the soup and let cook for another 20 minutes on a low fire or until the meat is done.

Rub dried mint in the palm of your hands to make it powdery. Add cinnamon and pepper to the mint. Add this to the soup just before removing it from the fire.

Taste soup, and if needed add more salt and lime juice for

 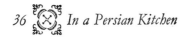

the right flavoring. If the pomegranate is sweet it will require
lime juice. *Makes 5–6 servings.*

Soupe Mast va Khiar

Cold Yogurt Soup

The first dish I learned to make was Soupe Mâst va Khiâr.
This is one of those soups which every family prepares differ-
ently. I learned the secret of this very soothing soup from my
mother and through years of practice have added my own
variations to it.

The basis for this soup is the famous yogurt. The combination of ingredients may sound odd and it is perhaps hard for
the average American to imagine that this soup could taste
good. But every summer I serve this soup at least a hundred
times, and I have yet to see one American who hasn't liked it
or who hasn't asked for seconds or even thirds.

Soupe Mâst va Khiâr is really a meal in itself. It is easy to
prepare and keeps for several days in the icebox without losing
its flavor or taste. On the contrary, it tastes better after staying
in the icebox for several hours. I am sure that if you prepare
this soup for family and friends you will be a very popular
housewife.

Cold Yogurt Soup

1 *boiled egg (chopped)*	1/4 *cup green onions (chopped)*
1/2 *cup raisins*	2 *tsp. salt*
2–3 *cups yogurt*	1/2 *tsp. pepper*
1/2 *cup light cream*	1 *cup cold water*
6 *ice cubes*	1 *tbsp. parsley (chopped)*
1 *cucumber (chopped)*	1 *tbsp. fresh dill (chopped)* or 1 *tsp. dill weed*

Soak the raisins in cold water for 5 minutes. Put yogurt in a big mixing bowl, add cream, chopped egg, ice cubes, chopped cucumber, green onions, salt, and pepper. Pour off the water from the raisins and add it to the yogurt mixture. Add 1 cup of cold water and mix well. Let this soup stand in the icebox for 2 to 3 hours. When serving, garnish with parsley and dill.

Makes 4–5 servings.

Ashe Mast

Hot Yogurt Soup

1/2 *lb. ground beef*	1 1/2 *tsp. salt*
1 *small onion (grated)*	1/2 *tsp. pepper*
1/2 *tsp. salt*	4 1/2 *cups water*
1/2 *tsp. pepper*	1/2 *cup parsley (chopped)*
4 *cups yogurt*	1/2 *cup green onions (chopped)*
1/4 *cup rice*	1/2 *tbsp. dill (optional)*
1 *egg*	1/2 *cup chick peas (canned)*
1 *tbsp. flour*	

Put the meat in a bowl. Add grated onion and seasoning and mix well. Make meat balls the size of walnuts. Put yogurt in a 3-quart pot. Add rice, egg, flour, and seasoning and beat well. Add water and mix. Cook over a very low fire, stirring constantly for about 20 minutes or until it thickens. Add meat balls to the yogurt mixture and let simmer for 10 minutes. Add vegetables and chick peas and let simmer for 15 minutes. Stir it often to avoid curdling.

Chop one or two cloves of garlic and sauté it in butter, add dried powdered mint, about 1 tablespoon, and put a teaspoonful of this hot garlic sauce on each plate of yogurt soup when serving. *Makes 6–7 servings.*

Ashe Reshte

Noodle Soup

I shall never forget how Ashe Reshte used to be prepared at our house in Persia. It was indeed a ritual. Our cook Ahmad used to get up early in the morning, prepare the dough for the noodles, cut the dough in the required size and shape, and let it stand in order to dry. Then he would set out for the bazaar, to do the daily shopping for lunch. In Persia, like most of the Middle Eastern countries, there is no refrigeration in the homes. Therefore, the Persian housewife is obliged to make arrangements for the daily shopping. She plans her meals carefully with the cook, and the cook starts his daily chores by visiting each shop for the needed ingredients.

Since Ashe Reshte was the family favorite, Ahmad didn't mind the routine. On the contrary, the daily shopping, visiting the various stores, and bargaining with the storekeepers was his favorite occupation. Ahmad's recipe of Ashe Reshte, I think, was one of the best I have ever eaten. In this book I have tried to simplify the method of preparing Ashe Reshte, yet have tried to retain the exact flavoring that used to be Ahmad's specialty.

Noodle Soup

1/2 *lb. ground beef*	1 *cup noodles*
1 *small onion (grated)*	1/2 *tsp. pepper*
1/4 *tsp. cinnamon*	1/2 *cup parsley (chopped)*
1/4 *tsp. pepper*	
1/2 *tsp. salt*	SPICING OF SOUP
4–5 *cups water*	
1 1/2 *tsp. salt*	1 *tbsp. dried mint*
1/4 *cup black-eyed peas*	1/4 *tsp. pepper*
1/4 *cup lentils*	1/4 *tsp. cinnamon*

Put the meat in a bowl. Add grated onions and seasoning, mix well and make meat balls the size of walnuts. Put the water in a 3-quart pot. Add salt and black-eyed peas and let cook for 15 minutes. Add meat balls, lentils, noodles, pepper, and parsley and let simmer on a medium fire for about 35 minutes.

Rub dried mint in the palm of your hands to make it powdery. Add cinnamon and pepper to the mint. Add this to the soup just before removing it from the fire. *Makes 5–6 servings.*

Ashe Torsh

Dried Fruit Soup

I remember my grandmother telling me, "Never eat Ashe Torsh when you have a cold or sore throat, but eat it if you want to keep a good and healthy constitution."

Ashe Torsh I believe is my family recipe. As long as I can remember, my grandmother and, after her, my mother made the best and the most delicately flavored Ashe Torsh. We were natives of Azerbaijan, and I think that this soup was more or less a family recipe from that region. Azerbaijan, located in the northwestern part of Iran, is very well known for its products of dried fruit. An Azerbaijani housewife knows many ways of using dried fruit in cooking. This soup is a favorite winter soup when dried fruit and nuts are available.

I have served Ashe Torsh many times to my American friends and have never failed to notice a surprised look on their faces. They always ask for seconds and if I don't hasten to tell them that there is another dish coming they will ask for a third helping. Ashe Torsh is a meal in itself. It is very satisfying and has an unusual sweet-and-sour taste flavored with mint and cinnamon. As any soup, it tastes better the day after it is made.

Dried Fruit Soup

1/2 lb. ground beef
1 small onion (grated)
1/4 tsp. cinnamon
1/4 tsp. pepper
1/2 tsp. salt
8 cups water
3 tsp. salt
1/2 cup rice
1 small onion (chopped fine)
2 tbsp. butter
1 cup dried prunes
1 cup dried apricots

1/4 cup walnuts (chopped)
1 cup parsley (chopped)
1/4 cup chick peas (canned)
1/2 cup vinegar
1/3 cup sugar

SPICING OF SOUP

1 tbsp. dried mint
1/4 tsp. cinnamon
1/4 tsp. pepper

Put the meat in a bowl. Add grated onions and seasoning and mix well. Make small meat balls the size of walnuts. Put water in a 3-quart pot. Add salt and rice and cook for 15 minutes. Meanwhile sauté chopped onions in butter and put them aside. Add prunes to the water and rice and let cook for another 15 minutes. Add meat balls, apricots, walnuts, parsley, and sautéed onions and let cook for about 20 minutes on a medium fire. Add vinegar and sugar and let cook on a medium fire for 15 minutes more.

Rub dried mint in the palm of your hands to make it powdery. Add cinnamon and pepper to the mint. Add this to the soup just before removing it from the fire. If more seasoning is necessary add to taste. *Makes 5–6 servings.*

"When cooks are many, the food is spoiled."
ARAB WISDOM

Eshkaneh

Onion Soup

5 tbsp. shortening
4 medium onions (sliced)
3 tbsp. flour
6 cups water
1/2 tsp. pepper
1 1/2 tsp. salt
1/2 tsp. turmeric
1/2 cup lime and lemon juice

1/3 cup sugar
2 eggs

SPICING OF SOUP

1 tbsp. dried mint
1/4 tsp. cinnamon
1/4 tsp. pepper

Melt shortening in a large pot. Add sliced onions and sauté for 5 minutes. Dissolve 3 tablespoons flour in a cup of water and add it to the sautéed onions. Add 5 cups of water and seasoning and let simmer on a low fire for 35 minutes. Mix sugar and lime and lemon juice and add it to the soup and let simmer for another 10 minutes. Rub dried mint in the palm of your hands to make it powdery. Add cinnamon and pepper to the mint. Add this to the soup just before removing it from the fire. Beat 2 eggs and add it to the soup just before serving.

Makes 5–6 servings.

Gushe Barreh

Persian Ravioli

I don't quite know when and how my family began preparing this soup. Perhaps my grandmother taught my mother or perhaps my mother picked it up in her travels through the northern part of Persia and the Caucasus. All I know is that as long as I can remember Gushe Barreh has been another favorite soup of my family. Mother used to make this soup at least once a week, and I remember that everybody showed up for lunch on that day. She used to prepare this soup on cold winter days, when it was most welcomed by the male members of the family.

Gushe Barreh is really very easy to prepare and, if you want a light dinner or lunch, it is a meal in itself. The combination of meat and dough cooked in water and seasoned with mint, cinnamon, and parsley and served with vinegar makes a very delightful meal.

1 *cup flour*	1/4 *tsp. pepper*
1/4 *tsp. salt*	1 *tsp. salt*
1/3 *cup water*	4 *cups water*
1/2 *lb. ground lamb*	1/4 *cup parsley (chopped)*
1 *small onion (grated)*	1 *tsp. dried mint*
1/4 *tsp. cinnamon*	1/4 *tsp. cinnamon*

Sift flour and salt into a bowl. Make a hollow in the center

of the flour. Add water gradually and mix with fork or hands until the dough is well mixed. Turn dough on a lightly floured board and knead well until dough is smooth. Put dough in the bowl, cover with a dish towel and let dough stand for 10 minutes.

Put beef or ground lamb in a bowl, add grated onions and seasoning and mix well.

Divide dough into workable parts. Roll dough on a floured board in a circular shape about 12 to 14 inches in diameter and cut into squares of 1 1/2" by 1 1/2". Put 1/2 teaspoonful meat in the center of each square and place another square on top (like a sandwich). Pinch the four edges together well with fingers or fork. Repeat this until the dough is finished.

Boil water with salt and pour the meat-filled squares in the water. Let boil for about 15 minutes or until done. Mix cinnamon and mint together. Right before removing the soup from the fire, add chopped parsley, mint, and cinnamon mixture. Serve with vinegar to taste. Some people like to eat this soup with yogurt. *Makes 5–6 servings.*

"*Three things are no disgrace to man—
to serve his guest, to serve his horse,
and to serve in his own house.*"
ARAB WISDOM

Stuffed Vegetables
and Fruits

Dolmeh Barg

Stuffed Grape Leaves

Dolmeh, which in Persian means "stuffed," usually stands for any kind of vegetable and fruit stuffed with meat and rice. Dolmeh Barg, which means literally "stuffed leaves," is the name for stuffed grape leaves. This is a real favorite of the Middle Eastern people as well as of the people of the Caucasus and Armenia.

It is difficult to trace the origin of this dish. Whether it originated in the vine-growing regions of the Caucasus or in the Middle East is subject to argument. Whatever its origin, it is the favorite dish of Turkomans, Tajiks, Uzbeks, Azerbaijanis, Armenians, Turks, Greeks, Arabs, and Persians, and last but not least it is the most popular dish among my American friends.

I cannot begin to count how many times I have made Dolmeh Barg and served it to my friends. It is so popular with them that they often phone to tell me they are coming for Dolmeh. Or they write a special-delivery letter saying that they are arriving in town and want Dolmeh for dinner. I really don't blame my friends for liking this dish so much, for it is truly the most exotic food you have ever tasted. When properly made, it acquires a very delicate taste from cooking the grape leaves in lemon juice and water.

There are many ways of preparing Dolmeh. It can be served cold or warm. When served warm, I prefer to stuff it with meat and vegetables. When served cold, I usually stuff it with rice and currants. However, when Dolmeh is stuffed with meat and vegetables, it tastes equally good when served cold.

Dolmeh makes excellent hors d'oeuvres for cocktails. It can be prepared a few days in advance, stored in the icebox, and cooked the day you are going to serve it. At first reading, this recipe may sound very complicated to you, but do try it. Dolmeh isn't really hard to make, and, with practice, you acquire the technique. And needless to say, Dolmeh makes an excellent topic for conversation at cocktail parties and dinners.

Stuffed Grape Leaves

50 *grape leaves (see p. 169)*
2/3 *cup rice (Minute Rice)*
1 *lb. ground beef*
1/2 *cup finely chopped green onions*
1/2 *cup finely chopped parsley*
1 *cup finely chopped celery leaves*
1/2 *cup finely chopped dill (optional)*

1 1/4 *tsp. salt*
1/2 *tsp. pepper*
1/2 *tsp. cinnamon*
2 *tbsp. butter (melted)*
2 1/2 *cups water*
4 *tbsp. lemon juice*

Put the grape leaves in a collander, wash with cold water, and drain. Cover the rice with cold water and soak for 5 minutes. Put the meat in a bowl. Add the chopped vegetables, seasoning, and melted butter. Drain the water from the rice and add to the meat mixture. Mix well (mixing by hand is more satisfactory). Take a grape leaf and put the vein side up on a cutting board. Nip off the little stem. Put a tablespoon of the meat mixture on the grape leaf. Fold the stem end over the meat, then the two sides toward the center and roll up. (With a little practice this folding process will become easy. The amount of meat will vary with the size of the leaf.) Arrange the rolled leaves in layers on the bottom of a 2-quart pot which has been lined with several unstuffed leaves. Pour 2-cups of water and the lemon juice over them. Put a small plate over the rolled leaves. Cover and let cook for about 1 1/2 hours or until tender. Serve with yogurt.

If fresh grape leaves are used, pick small tender ones. Wash the leaves in boiling water for 10 minutes until the leaves become tender. Dolmeh may be cooked in a pressure cooker in about 10 minutes. *Makes 6 servings.*

Yalanci Dolma

Rice Stuffed Grape Leaves

50 *grape leaves*	1 1/4 *tsp. salt*
1 1/4 *cups olive oil and Wesson oil mixed*	1/2 *tsp. pepper*
3 1/2 *cups onions (finely chopped)*	1/2 *tsp. cinnamon*
1 1/2 *cups rice*	1/2 *tsp. allspice*
1 *cup chopped dill*	1/2 *cup water*
1/2 *cup currants*	3 *tbsp. lemon juice*
	2 *cups water*

Put the grape leaves in a collander, wash with cold water,

and drain. Cover the rice with cold water and soak for 5 minutes. Put half the oil in a skillet and heat it. Add chopped onions and rice and sauté on a medium fire for about 15 minutes or until the onions and the rice are lightly golden. Add chopped parsley, dill and currants, and seasoning. Sauté for another 5 minutes. Add the rest of the oil and 1/2 cup of water. Cover and let simmer for about 25 minutes or until the rice is tender. Let cool. Take a grape leaf and put the vein side up on a cutting board. Nip off the little stem. Put a tablespoon of rice mixture on the grape leaf. Fold the stem end over the rice, then the two sides toward the center and roll up. The amount of the filling will vary with the size of the leaf. Arrange the rolled leaves in layers on the bottom of a 2-quart pot which has been lined with several unstuffed leaves. Pour 2 cups of water and lemon juice over them. Put a small plate over the leaves. Cover and let cook for about 1 hour or until tender. Remove pot and let cool. Arrange the stuffed leaves on a plate and put it in the refrigerator until ready to serve. Serve cold with slices of lemon. *Makes 4–5 servings.*

Stuffed Eggplants

Dolmeh Bâdemjân is one of those dishes that everybody

should prepare at least once in order to realize what a delicious and exquisite vegetable eggplant can be.

My family has always been fond of stuffed eggplants, and therefore my mother has tried to find the best way of preparing them. In this book I am giving you two ways of preparing Dolmeh Bâdemjân. Basically they are the same. They both consist of eggplants stuffed with ground meat, seasoned, and mixed with yellow split peas or, sometimes, cooked rice. It is only the sauce in which they are cooked that varies. You can either prepare them in tomato sauce or cook them with sweet-and-sour sauce. The final results of both are very delicious. Each is a meal in itself.

Stuffed Eggplants with Tomato Sauce

4 *medium eggplants*	1/4 *tsp. nutmeg*
1/3 *cup yellow split peas*	1/2 *tsp. cinnamon*
1 *cup water*	2 *tbsp. chopped parsley*
1 *lb. ground beef*	2 *tbsp. shortening*
1 *large onion (finely chopped)*	1 *cup tomato sauce*
2 *tbsp. butter*	1/2 *cup water*
1 *tsp. salt*	3 *tbsp. lemon juice*
1/4 *tsp. pepper*	

Wash eggplants. Cut a thin slice from each stem and save them. Remove the pulp with apple corer. Wash inside of the eggplants well. Salt inside, let stay for 20 minutes (this process takes away the bitterness). Cook split peas in water for 30 minutes. Meanwhile, sauté the beef and the onions in butter. Combine meat and split peas. Add seasoning and parsley. Wash the inside of the eggplants once more to remove the salt. Fill the eggplants with the meat mixture. Put the thin slices back on the top so that the stuffing doesn't come out. Sauté the eggplants lightly in shortening for 10 minutes. Add tomato sauce, water, and lemon juice. Cover and simmer on a low fire for 30 minutes. Serve the eggplants with their own sauce and yogurt. *Makes 4 servings.*

Sweet-and-Sour Stuffed Eggplants

4 *small eggplants*	1/4 *tsp. pepper*
2 *green peppers*	1/4 *cup rice (Minute Rice)*
1/3 *cup yellow split peas*	1/2 *cup parsley (finely chopped)*
1 1/2 *cups water*	1/4 *cup leek or green onions (finely*
1 *large onion (finely chopped)*	*chopped)*
2 *tbsp. butter*	2 *cups water*
1 *lb. ground beef*	1/2 *cup vinegar*
1 *tsp. salt*	1/3 *cup sugar*
1/2 *tsp. cinnamon*	1 *tbsp. saffron*

Wash eggplants. Cut thin slices from each stem and save them. Remove the pulp with apple corer. Wash inside of the eggplants well. Salt the inside and let stay for 20 minutes (this process takes away the bitterness of the eggplants). Use the same process for the green peppers. Cook yellow split peas in water for 30 minutes or until they are done. Sauté the onions in butter and put them aside. Put meat in a bowl, add seasoning, rice, parsley, leek, yellow split peas, and sautéed onions and mix well. Fill the eggplants and the green pepper with the meat mixture. Put the thin slices back on the top so that the stuffing doesn't come out. Put the eggplants and peppers in a pot. Add water and let cook on a medium fire for about 25 minutes. Mix

vinegar and sugar and saffron and add this to the eggplant and pepper and let simmer for another 25 minutes.

Makes 4–5 servings.

Dolmeh Felfel Sabz va Gojeh Farangi

Stuffed Green Peppers and Tomatoes

4 *green peppers*	1 *medium onion (finely chopped)*
1 *cup water*	1 *lb. ground beef*
1 *tsp. salt*	1 1/4 *tsp. salt*
3 *large tomatoes*	1/4 *tsp. pepper*
1/4 *cup rice*	1/2 *tsp. cinnamon*
1/4 *cup yellow split peas*	2 *tbsp. butter*
2 1/2 *cups water*	2 *tbsp. tomato sauce*
2 *tbsp. butter*	*tomato pulp and juice*

Wash peppers. Cut thin slice from stem end of each and save them. Remove seeds. Boil water with salt. Put peppers in the water and let them boil for 5 minutes. Drain and put them aside. Cut thin slice from stem end of each tomato. Save these. Scoop out pulp and juice from tomatoes. Save pulp and juice.

Cook rice and yellow split peas in water for 25 minutes or until done. If your rice takes a long time to cook, cook them separately. Melt butter in a skillet and sauté onions and meat for 10 minutes. Put meat mixture in a bowl, add cooked rice and yellow split peas, parsley, green onions, and seasoning. Mix well. If more seasoning is needed, add to taste. Lightly fill the green peppers and tomatoes with meat mixture. Put stems back so that the meat doesn't fall out. Melt butter in a skillet. Arrange peppers and tomatoes in the skillet. Add tomato sauce and pulp and juice. Cover and let cook on a low fire for 20–35 minutes or until done. Serve topped with yogurt.

Makes 4–5 servings.

Dolmeh Kadu

Stuffed Squash

5–6 *summer squash*	1 *lb. ground beef*
1/3 *cup yellow split peas*	1 *tsp. salt*
1 1/2 *cups water*	1/4 *tsp. pepper*
2 *tbsp. butter*	1/2 *tsp. cinnamon*
1 *onion (finely chopped)*	1/2 *cup water*

Wash squash. Cut thin slices from stem of each and remove pulp with apple corer. Cook yellow split peas in water for 30 minutes or until they are done. Sauté the onion in butter and put it aside. Sauté the meat with seasoning until it is golden brown. Let cool. Add yellow split peas to the meat and mix well. If it needs more seasoning, add to taste. Fill squash with the meat mixture. Arrange the squash in a skillet. Add water

 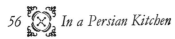

and let simmer on a low fire for 20 minutes or until done. Serve topped with yogurt. *Makes 4–5 servings.*

Dolmeh Kalam

Stuffed Cabbage Leaves

Dolmeh Kalam seems to be an international dish. I have found this dish popular among my friends, both Western and Eastern. In Persia too, this dish is a rather popular one and, of course, it has the special Persian touch in seasoning.

In this book, I have given you two ways of preparing stuffed cabbage. One is with tomato sauce and the other with sweet-and-sour sauce. I think you should try them both. However, the sweet-and-sour sauce is the special family recipe and favorite of mine and my American friends which I think you should try first.

Stuffed Cabbage Leaves with Sweet-and-Sour Sauce

1 *large head of cabbage*	1/4 *tsp. pepper*
1/4 *cup yellow split peas*	1/2 *tsp. cinnamon*
1 *cup water*	1 *tsp. salt*
1 *lb. ground beef*	1 1/2 *cups water*
1 *medium onion (finely chopped)*	1/3 *cup sugar*
1/4 *cup rice (Minute Rice)*	1/2 *cup vinegar*
1/2 *cup parsley (chopped)*	

Core cabbage, set it in a pot of boiling salted water, cover, and cook until almost tender (be careful not to overcook it). Drain well and remove leaves, cut out midribs. Cook yellow split peas in water for 30 minutes or until cooked. Put ground beef in a bowl. Add onions, rice, parsley, cooked split peas, and seasoning and mix well. Take each leaf in your hand and put a tablespoon of meat mixture on it. Shape into finger-shaped packages. Line the bottom of a pan with cabbage leaves that couldn't be used. Pack in stuffed leaves, placing any remaining leaves between layers. Pour water on the cabbage and cook on a low fire for 35 minutes. Mix sugar and vinegar and pour over the cabbage and let cook for another 20 minutes.

Makes 4–5 servings.

Stuffed Cabbage Leaves with Tomato Sauce

1 *large head of cabbage*	1 *cup rice (Minute Rice)*
3 *tbsp. butter*	1 *cup water*
1 *lb. stew beef, cut in 1/2" cubes*	1/2 *tbsp. salt*
1 *onion (finely chopped)*	1/4 *cup parsley (chopped)*
1 *tsp. salt*	1 *tbsp. fresh or dry dill*
1/4 *tsp. pepper*	1/2 *cup tomato sauce*
1/4 *tsp. cinnamon*	1/2 *cup water*
1/2 *cup tomato sauce*	2 *tbsp. lemon juice*
1/2 *cup water*	

Core cabbage, set it in a pot of boiling salted water, cover, and cook until almost tender (be careful not to overcook it). Drain well and remove leaves, cut out midribs. Melt shortening. Sauté meat with onions and seasoning until golden brown. Add tomato sauce and water and let simmer for 25 minutes. Cook rice with water and salt according to the directions on

 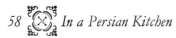

the box. Put the meat and the cooked rice in a bowl. Add chopped parsley, dill and mix well. If a little more salt is required, add to taste. Take each leaf in your hand. Put a tablespoonful of meat mixture on it and shape it into a finger-shaped package. Line the bottom of the pan with the cabbage leaves that couldn't be used. Pack in stuffed leaves, placing any remaining leaves between layers. Pour tomato sauce and water and lemon juice over cabbage leaves. Cover with inverted plate and pot lid. Cook over a low heat for 45 minutes to 1 hour. Serve topped with yogurt.   *Makes 4–5 servings.*

Dolmeh Beh

Stuffed Quince

Beh, or quince, is not well known in America. The few people who have heard of this fruit know only that one makes jam or jelly out of it.

The Persian housewife not only knows how to prepare a very excellent jam out of quince, but she also has found other extraordinary uses for it. Every Persian housewife will try to prepare stuffed quince when this delicate fruit is in season. I have eaten this dolmeh in many Persian homes. However, I believe that this family recipe is one of the best Dolmeh Beh that I have ever tasted. The proportion of the sweet-and-sour seasoning is what brings out the real taste of the quince. I think you should try it at least once. I am sure you will enjoy it and you will create a topic of conversation for your guests.

Stuffed Quince

6–7 *quinces*	1 *tsp. salt*
1/4 *cup yellow split peas*	1/4 *tsp. pepper*
1 1/2 *cups water*	1/2 *tsp. cinnamon*
2 *tbsp. butter*	3/4 *cup water*
1 *medium onion (finely chopped)*	1/3 *cup vinegar*
1 *lb. ground beef*	1/2 *cup sugar*

Wash the quinces well but do not peel them. Cut thin slices from the stem of each and save them. Remove the pulp with apple corer and make a cavity large enough for stuffing. Cook yellow split peas in water for 30 minutes or until they are done. Sauté onions in butter until golden. Put them aside. Sauté the meat until done. Let cool. Add onions, seasoning, and yellow split peas to the meat and mix well. Stuff this filling into the quinces and place them side by side in a pan. Add some water and do not allow the water to come up higher than 1″. Cover the pan and let it come to a boil. Lower fire and let simmer on a very low fire for 30 minutes or until the quinces are tender. The time necessary for cooking depends on the size of the quinces. Meanwhile, mix vinegar and sugar and let boil for a few minutes. Just before the quinces are entirely done, baste them with the vinegar mixture and let simmer for another 15 minutes. Serve the quinces with the sweet-and-sour sauce which is in the pan. *Makes 5–6 servings.*

Dolmeh Sib

Stuffed Apples

I have already mentioned that the Persians are masters of combining fresh fruit with meat. Dolmeh Sib is a true delicacy among the dolmeh family. If you eat Dolmeh Sib once, you will never forget the delicate flavor created by the combination of apples stuffed with meat and onions and the right seasoning.

I believe it is the combination of sweet-and-sour seasoning in which the apples are baked that gives Dolmeh Sib its exquisite flavoring. Dolmeh Sib is a dish which can be prepared the year round in America. It is a very satisfying meal, easy to prepare, and quite a unique dish with which to surprise your guests.

8–10 *apples*
1/3 *cup yellow split peas*
1 1/2 *cups water*
2 *tbsp. butter*
1 *onion (finely chopped)*
1 *lb. ground beef*
1 *tsp. salt*

1/2 *tsp. cinnamon*
1/4 *tsp. pepper*
1 *tbsp. butter*
1/4 *cup vinegar*
1/4 *cup water*
3 *tbsp. sugar*

Wash apples well. Cut thin slices from the stem of each and save them. Remove the pulp with apple corer. Cook yellow split peas in water for 30 minutes or until they are done. Sauté the onions in butter and put them aside. Sauté meat until golden brown. Let cool. Add onions and split peas to the meat and mix well. If seasoning is needed, add more to taste. Fill the apples with meat mixture and put the thin slices back on the top so that stuffing doesn't come out. Arrange the apples in a baking pan and bake in a 350° preheated oven for 1/2 hour. Put vinegar, water, sugar, and butter together in a pot and bring to a boil over a medium fire. When the apples are half done, remove the apples from the oven, lift the top of each apple, and baste it with vinegar mixture. Return apples to the oven and let cook until they are done. Serve apples with sweet and-sour sauce in the baking pan. *Makes 6–8 serving.*

"*It is of my ways that a man shall come out with his guest to the door of my house.*"

MOHAMMAD

Pilafs

For generations the Iranians and the Near Easterners have used rice, or *berenj*, as a basic food. It is the daily staple for all, and the bread and potatoes of Iran and her neighboring countries.

The Iranian farmer takes great pride in his rice fields and produces the most delicately flavored rice known. Most of the long-grain rice which is grown in Iran comes from the Caspian Sea area, the provinces of Gilan and Mazandaran, and the slopes of the Alborz Mountains. A small quantity for local consumption is also grown on the plateau in a few localities where an abundant supply of water is available.

There are three well-known varieties of rice in Iran. First is Berenje Domsiâh, second Berenje Sadri, and third, Berenje Champâ, indicated in the order of their quality.

Since rice is the daily food of the people of Iran, the Iranian housewife, through years of practice, has developed a special method of cooking the rice in order to preserve all its natural flavor and produce a light and fluffy delicacy. She calls this fluffy rice *polo* or *pilâf*, as it is better known in the West. Americans serve their basic food, potatoes, in many ways, fried, baked, or mashed. And, like the American housewife, the Iranian housewife has also learned to prepare polo in many ways. The more ways she knows how to prepare polo the better she has captured the art of cooking this delicate dish.

The preparation of polo is indeed an art, and I believe that the Persians are the connoisseurs of this art. Although rice has been known as the product of China and India, the only way the people of these countries know how to prepare rice is by just plain boiling it. But the Persians, who have introduced the art of cooking rice to their neighboring countries, consider polo as the essence of an exquisite dinner, steaming it and using other various methods which will be discussed.

Persians have two basic ways of serving rice, either as *chelo* or as *polo*.

Chelo is the name applied to steamed white rice cooked separately and "over" which different types of sauces and/or meats are served.

Polo, often called pilâf in America, is the name applied to rice "with" which other ingredients are mixed in the cooking process.

Chelo

Steamed Rice

2 1/2 *cups rice*	2 *tbsp. salt*
1 1/2 *tbsp. salt*	1/2 *cup butter (melted)*
2 *qts. water*	

Step by Step Method

1). Wash rice three times in lukewarm water and then soak in cold water to which 1 1/2 tablespoons of salt have been added. Use enough cold water to cover the rice. This rice should be soaked overnight (in a pinch, 1 or 2 hours' soaking will suffice).

2). Boil 2 quarts of water to which 2 tablespoons of salt have been added.

3). Pour off the water in which the rice has been soaked. Add rice to the boiling water and boil it for 10–15 minutes. (Stir rice with spoon once or twice to prevent the grains from sticking together.)

4). Pour the rice and water into a strainer and rinse with luke-warm water.

5). Put 1/3 of the melted butter into the bottom of the pot in which you cooked the rice. Add 2 tablespoons of water to the butter in the pot.

6). Take a spoonful of rice at a time and put it in the pot, distributing it evenly. Allow it to mount into the shape of a cone.

7). Pour the rest of the melted butter over the rice, distributing it evenly.

8). Put paper toweling over the pot. Cover and put 2 or 3 dishtowels on the lid. Cook for 10–15 minutes on medium fire. Lower the fire and cook for 35–40 minutes on low fire.

If the rice is cooked at the right temperature, the rice will form a crust at the bottom of the pot which will become crisp and turn a golden brown, while the rest of the rice remains white. If desired, add more melted butter before serving.

Makes 4 servings.

[Note] Put the pot in the sink filled with cold water for a few minutes before serving. This process makes it easy to remove the crust. By putting dishtowels over the lid the rice will cook more evenly throughout.

When serving rice, put 2–3 tablespoons of rice in a dish and add to it 2 tablespoons of saffron (see p. 170). Mix it well and decorate the chelo with this rice. Saffron gives chelo a nice color and flavor.

Chelo is served with various types of *khoreshes* or sauces.

Kateh

Cooked Rice

Kateh, slightly different from chelo or polo, is a popular dish among the people of the Caspian Sea region. Since these people eat rice practically three times a day, they have learned to cook it in various easy ways. The preparation of kateh, as directions will indicate, is much easier than that of chelo or polo. Kateh is economical and quick to prepare.

2 *cups rice*	1 *tbsp. butter*
4 *cups water*	2 *tbsp. shortening*
1 1/2 *tsp. salt*	

Measure 2 cups of rice, wash, and drain well. Put rice in a 2-quart pot. Add 3 cups of water and salt. Cover. Let cook on a medium fire for about 30 minutes or until the water is absorbed. Stir the rice a few times while it is boiling. When rice is cooked, add butter and shortening. Cover and let cook about 35 minutes on a low medium fire.

When ready to serve, fill your sink halfway with cold water. Put the pot in the sink for a few minutes and remove. Take a spatula and invert the cooked rice on a plate. The finished product should look crisp and brown on top.

Kateh can be served with any of the *khoreshes* or sauces (to be discussed under sauces). It can be served with broiled meats or just plain fried eggs. *Makes 3–4 servings.*

Adas Polo

Rice with Lentils

2 *tbsp. butter*	1/2 *cup raisins*
1 *lb. meat (shoulder of lamb cut up, beef or lamb stew-meat cut into 1" cubes)*	1 1/2 *tbsp. butter*
	3/4 *cup lentils*
	2 1/2 *cups rice*
1 *medium onion (finely chopped)*	1 1/2 *tbsp. salt*
1/2 *tsp. salt*	2 *qt. water*
1/4 *tsp. pepper*	2 *tbsp. salt*
1/4 *tsp. nutmeg*	1/2 *cup butter (melted)*
1/2 *tsp. cinnamon*	

Melt butter in a skillet. Sauté the meat with the onions and seasoning. Wash and soak the raisins in cold water for 5

minutes. Cook the rice and lentils as in directions for chelo (see p. 65). (Do not soak the lentils, just soak the rice as directed.) When you come to step *6* of the directions for chelo, after putting half of the rice in the pot, arrange the meat and onions over the rice and the lentils and add the raisins. Add the rest of the rice and the lentils over the raisins. Cook as directed for chelo. As a variation ground beef can be substituted for lamb or beef cubes. *Makes 5–6 servings.*

Bagali Polo

Rice with Lima Beans

Many times American friends have asked me, "What is dill?" saying, "I have never eaten anything but dill pickles." It is very surprising how few people in the United States know of this very delicate herb. And those who know of it have very little knowledge of how to use it.

Iranians have favored dill for many years and use it in many dishes. One of these famous and extremely tasteful dishes is Bagali Polo, where dill is used in combination with rice and lima beans. This dish is the favorite of the people of Mazandaran as well as Tehran. It is prepared with lamb and is eaten with yogurt.

Rice with Lima Beans

2 1/2–3 lb. shoulder of lamb
2–3 tbsp. butter
1 large onion (finely chopped)
1/2 tsp. salt
1/4 tsp. pepper
1/4 tsp. cinnamon
1 pkg. frozen lima beans

1 cup finely chopped fresh dill or
    4–5 tbsp. dill weed
2 1/2 cups rice
1 1/2 tbsp. salt
2 qt. water
2 tbsp. salt
1/2 cup butter (melted)

Have the butcher cut the lamb shoulder into chops. Melt butter and sauté the onions until golden. Then put them aside. Sauté the meat with seasonings, until the meat is browned. Add water and let simmer about 30 minutes or until the meat is tender. Cook lima beans as directed on the box. Cook rice as in directions for chelo (see p. 65). When you come to step 6 of the directions for chelo put half of the rice in the pot, arrange the meat, half of the lima beans, and half of the dill over the rice. Add some more rice, then the rest of the lima beans and dill and remaining rice. Cook as directed for chelo. Sliced roast turkey, or left-over turkey, or other meats can be used instead of lamb. Serve this rice with yogurt.

Makes 4–5 servings.

"Woman is a torment, but, O God, let
no home be without it."
    PERSIAN PROVERB

Morg Polo

Rice with Chicken

It is strange how people associate a certain dish with a certain place or a certain occasion. As long as I can remember I have always associated Morg Polo with the Persian New Year's Eve, when my family would gather around a large table and celebrate this festive day. Even in America I have tried to maintain the old Persian tradition and serve Morg Polo on the eve of the Persian New Year. Morg Polo is a favorite chicken dish which an Iranian housewife serves on festive occasions such as weddings and holidays. Persians serve chicken for the same occasions that Americans serve turkey. If the Persian housewife has a guest, she will almost always serve some form of chicken.

A combination of chicken and raisins, cooked with rice and flavored with saffron when served, makes an extremely delicately flavored dish easily prepared. I have served this dish to many of my American friends on different occasions and I have found them always asking for this delicious recipe.

Rice with Chicken

2 1/2–3 lb. fryer (cut up)	1/2 cup dried apricots (chopped)
5 tbsp. butter	1 1/2 tbsp. butter
1 large onion (finely chopped)	2 1/2 cups rice
1 tsp. poultry seasoning	1 1/2 tbsp. salt
1 tsp. salt	2 qt. water
1/4 tsp. cinnamon	2 tbsp. salt
1/4 tsp. pepper	1/2 cup butter
2/3 cup seedless raisins or currants	

Clean and wash the fryer. Melt butter in a deep skillet. Sauté the onions until golden and put them aside. Then sauté the chicken with seasoning. Meanwhile wash and soak the raisins or currants in cold water for 5 minutes. Melt 1 1/2 tablespoons butter and sauté the raisins and apricots on a low fire for just a few minutes. Cook rice as in directions for chelo (see p. 65). When you come to step *6* of the directions for chelo, after putting half of the rice in the pot, arrange the fried chicken, onions, raisins, and apricots over the rice. Add the rest of the rice and cook as directed for chelo.

Makes 4–5 servings.

Sutti Polo

Rice with Milk

For many years the women of the northwestern part of

Iran, the province of Azerbaijan, have taken great pride in their homemaking and especially in their culinary art. An Azerbaijani woman is known all over Iran as a good cook. There is a saying that "If you marry an Azerbaijani woman you will eat well." She is noted for using great imagination in her cooking and for taking pride in the variety of dishes which she can prepare.

Sutti Polo is a favorite with the people of this area of Iran. The people of Azerbaijan speak Turkish, and the name of this dish is derived from the Turkish word *sutti*, meaning "with milk." Sutti Polo, as directions will indicate, is cooked with milk and dried fruit. It is a very economical and nourishing dish. Although it lacks meat, it contains all the necessary vitamins.

2 *cups rice*	1–2 *tbsp. butter*
3 *cups milk*	1/3 *cup raisins*
1 1/2 *tsp. salt*	2/3 *cup dates (seedless)*
1 *tsp. saffron (see p. 170)*	3 *tbsp. butter*

Wash and drain 2 cups of rice. Put the rice in a 2-quart pot. Add the milk, butter, salt, and saffron. Put the pot on a medium fire. Cook rice about 25 minutes or until the milk is absorbed. Stir rice a few times while cooking so that the rice will not stick to the bottom of the pan.

Meanwhile wash the raisins and dates. Melt butter in a skillet and sauté the raisins and dates for 5 minutes.

When the rice is done, make a little hole in the middle of the rice. Put the sautéed raisins and dates in the middle and cover it with rice. Put the butter on top and sides. Cover and cook over low fire about 30 minutes. Put the pot in a sink of cold water for a few minutes and then serve. (This process prevents the bottom of the rice from sticking to the pan.)

Makes 3–4 servings.

Shirini Polo

Sweet Rice

2 cups carrots, sliced in 1″ strips	1/4 tsp. pepper
1 cup water	1/2 tsp. poultry seasoning
4–5 tbsp. butter	2 tbsp. saffron (see p. 170)
1 cup almonds, blanched and sliced	2 1/2 cups rice
2–3 tbsp. butter	1 1/2 tbsp. salt
1/2 cup candied orange peel	2 qt. water
4–5 breasts of chicken	2 tbsp. salt
2/3 cup water	1/2 cup butter
1/2 tsp. salt	2 tbsp. saffron

Wash, clean, and quarter the carrots lengthwise and then cut into 1″ pieces. Cook the carrots in 1 cup water until the water is gone. Sauté the carrots in butter. Sauté the almonds in 3 tbsp. butter. Add candied orange to the sautéed carrots and let cook on a very low fire about 15–20 minutes. Parboil the chicken with the seasoning and saffron for 20–25 minutes. Cook rice as in directions for chelo (see p. 65). When you come to step *6* of the directions for chelo, after putting half the rice in the pot, arrange half of the chicken, half of the carrots

 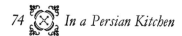

and orange peel, and half of the almonds over the rice. Add some more rice, chicken, then the rest of the orange peel, carrots, and almonds and the remaining rice. When ready to serve, add the 2 tablespoons of saffron to the rice and mix.

Makes 4–5 servings.

Tah Chin

Rice and Lamb

Tah Chin, which in Persian means "arranged at the bottom of the pot," is a very tasty and exotic dish. This dish derives its name from the way the baked lamb is arranged at the bottom of the pot. Lamb meat, contrary to the popular belief in America, is a very delicate meat when marinated in yogurt and properly seasoned. This dish is a popular one with the housewives of Tehran.

3–4 *lb. leg or shoulder of lamb, trimmed*	1 *egg*
2 *cups yogurt*	1 *tsp. saffron*
1/4 *tsp. cinnamon*	2 1/2 *cups rice*
1/4 *tsp. pepper*	1 1/2 *tbsp. salt*
1/2 *tsp. salt*	2 *qt. water*
1 *tsp. saffron (see p. 170)*	2 *tbsp. salt*
	1/2 *cup butter*

Marinate the meat in the yogurt and the four seasonings for

3 to 4 hours. Remove lamb from yogurt. Put the meat in a casserole and bake it in a 375° oven for about 30 minutes. Meanwhile add 1 egg and another teaspoon of saffron to the yogurt in which the meat was being marinated. Cook rice as in directions for chelo (see p. 65). When you come to step *6* of the directions for chelo, take 5 to 6 tablespoons rice and mix it with the yogurt mixture and line the bottom of the pan with this rice. Arrange the baked meat over the rice and pour the rest of the rice over the meat. Cover and cook as directed for chelo.   *Makes 5–6 servings.*

Estanboli Polo

Rice with Tomato Sauce

4 *tbsp. butter*	2/3 *cup tomato sauce*
1 *lb. ground beef or stew meat, cut into 1/2" cubes*	1/2 *cup water*
	2–3 *tbsp. lemon juice*
1 *medium onion (finely chopped)*	2 1/2 *cups rice*
1/2 *tsp. salt*	1 1/2 *tbsp. salt*
1/4 *tsp. pepper*	2 *qt. water*
1/4 *tsp. cinnamon*	2 *tbsp. salt*
1/4 *tsp. paprika*	1/2 *cup butter (melted)*

Melt butter in a 3-quart pot. Add meat, onions, and seasonings and sauté until meat is brown. Add tomato sauce, water, and lemon juice and let simmer for 30 minutes on a medium fire or until the meat absorbs all the juice. Cook rice as in directions for chelo (see p. 65). When you come to step *6* of the directions for chelo, after putting half of the rice in the pot, place the meat and the sauce over the rice, pour the rest of the rice over the meat. Cook as directed for chelo.

Makes 4–5 servings.

Geisi Polo

Rice with Apricots

3 *tbsp. butter or shortening*	1/2 *cup raisins*
2 1/2–3 *lbs. shoulder of lamb*	2/3 *cup dried apricots*
1/2 *tsp. salt*	2 1/2 *cups rice*
1/3 *tsp. pepper*	1 1/2 *tbsp. salt*
1/4 *tsp. cinnamon*	2 *qt. water*
1/4 *tsp. nutmeg*	2 *tbsp. salt*
2/3 *cup water*	1/2 *cup butter (melted)*

Have the butcher cut the lamb shoulder into chops. Clean the lamb and trim the fat. Melt the butter in a skillet and sauté the lamb with the seasonings. Add water and let simmer on a low fire for 30 minutes. Quarter each of the apricots. Wash the raisins and the apricots. Melt butter in a skillet and sauté the apricots and the raisins about 5 minutes. Cook rice as in directions for chelo (see p. 65). When you come to step *6* of the directions for chelo, after putting half of the rice in the pot, arrange meat, apricots, and raisins over the rice. Pour the rest of the rice over the meat mixture. Cover and cook as directed for chelo. *Makes 4–5 servings.*

Tah Chine Esfanaj

Rice with Spinach

3–4 *lb. shoulder of lamb*	1/2 *cup yogurt*
4 *tbsp. butter*	1/2 *tsp. salt*
1/2 *tsp. salt*	1/4 *tsp. pepper*
1/4 *tsp. pepper*	1/4 *tsp. cinnamon*
1/2 *tsp. cinnamon*	1/2 *tsp. garlic salt*
1/2 *tsp. paprika*	1 *egg*
1 *tsp. saffron (see p. 170)*	2 1/2 *cups rice*
1 *lb. fresh spinach*	1 1/2 *tbsp. salt*
1 *cup water*	2 *qt. water*
1 *medium onion*	2 *tbsp. salt*
4 *tbsp. butter*	1/2 *cup butter*

Have the butcher cut the lamb shoulder into chops. Clean and trim the fat off the chops. Melt butter in a skillet. Sauté the chops with seasoning and saffron. Wash, clean, and chop the spinach. Boil the spinach in water for 8 minutes. Chop the onions and sauté them in butter. When the onions are half done, squeeze the water from the boiled spinach and sauté it with the onions. Pour the sautéed onions and spinach in yogurt. Season and mix well. Put the eggs in a bowl and beat well.

Cook rice as in directions for chelo (see p. 65). When you come to step 6 of the directions for chelo, before putting half of the rice in the pot, take 5 to 6 tablespoons of rice and mix it well with eggs. Line the bottom of the pan with this rice. Now pour the spinach and yogurt mixture and distribute evenly. Arrange the sautéed meat over the spinach. Pour the rest of the rice over the meat. Cover and cook as directed for chelo. This pilâf has an excellent flavor and forms a very tasty crust at the bottom. *Makes 5–6 servings.*

Havij Polo

Rice with Carrots

1 *lb. ground lamb or beef*	3 *tbsp. butter*
1 *medium onion (finely chopped)*	2 *tbsp. sugar*
1/2 *tsp. salt*	2 1/2 *cups rice*
1/4 *tsp. pepper*	1 1/2 *tbsp. salt*
1/4 *tsp. cinnamon*	2 *qt. water*
1/4 *tsp. paprika*	2 *tbsp. salt*
4 *tbsp. butter*	1/2 *cup butter (melted)*
6 *carrots*	

Put the meat in a bowl. Add onions and seasonings and mix well. Make into small balls the size of walnuts (makes 20–25 meat balls). Sauté the meat balls in butter. Peel the carrots and dice them. Sauté the carrots in butter for 15 minutes, add sugar, and let simmer for a few more minutes. Cook rice as in directions for chelo (see p. 65). When you come to step *6* of the directions for chelo, after putting half of the rice in the pot, arrange the meat over the rice. Pour the rest of the rice over the meat and put the carrots on top of the rice. Cook as directed for chelo. *Makes 4–5 servings.*

Kadu Polo

Rice with Pumpkin

1 *lb. ground beef or lamb*	2 1/2 *cups rice*
1 *medium onion (chopped very fine)*	1 1/2 *tbsp. salt*
1/2 *tsp. salt*	2 *qt. water*
1/4 *tsp. pepper*	2 *tbsp. salt*
1/2 *tsp. cinnamon*	1/2 *cup butter*
1 *small pumpkin*	

Put the meat in a bowl. Add chopped onions and seasoning and mix well. Make regular hamburger patties with this meat. Cut pumpkin in half and then in semicircles, 2″ in width (makes 7–8 semicircles). Peel these semicircles. Cook rice as in directions for chelo (see p. 65). When you come to step *6* of the directions for chelo, after putting about 6 tablespoons of rice in the pan, arrange the hamburgers on the top of this rice. Pour enough

rice to cover the hamburgers. Now arrange the pumpkins on this rice. (If the pumpkins are not sweet enough, add sugar to taste.) Pour the rest of the rice on the pumpkins. Cook according to directions for chelo. *Makes 5–6 servings.*

Reshte Polo

Rice with Noodles

3 *tbsp. butter*	2 *tbsp. butter*
1 *large onion (finely chopped)*	1/2 *cup raisins*
2 1/2–3 *lb. shoulder of lamb*	2/3 *cup very fine egg noodles*
1 *tsp. salt*	2 1/2 *cups rice*
1/2 *tsp. pepper*	1 1/2 *tbsp. salt*
1/2 *tsp. cinnamon*	2 *qt. water*
1/4 *tsp. nutmeg*	2 *tbsp. salt*
2/3 *cup water*	1/2 *cup butter*

Melt butter in a skillet. Sauté the onions, remove and set aside. Have the butcher cut the lamb shoulder into chops. Place the lamb in the skillet, add the seasoning, and sauté it until the meat is browned. Add the water and let simmer on a low fire for 30 minutes. Melt the butter in a skillet and sauté the raisins about 5 minutes. Toast the noodles in a skillet for about 5 minutes. Now follow step *3* in directions for chelo (see p. 65). Boil the noodles in the rice as directed. Follow these directions until step *6*. When you come to step *6* of the directions for chelo, after putting half the rice in the pot, arrange meat and sautéed onions over the rice and noodles. Pour the rest of the rice and noodles over the raisins. Cover and cook as directed for chelo.   *Makes 4-5 servings.*

Sabzi Polo

Rice with Vegetables

2 1/2-3 *lb. shoulder of lamb*
4 *tbsp. butter*
1/2 *tsp. salt*
1/4 *tsp. pepper*
1/2 *tsp. cinnamon*
1/4 *tsp. paprika*
1/4 *cup water*
1/2 *cup chopped green onions*

1/2 *cup chopped parsley*
1/2 *cup chopped celery leaves*
2 1/2 *cups rice*
1 1/2 *tbsp. salt*
2 *qt. water*
2 *tbsp. salt*
1/2 *cup butter*

Have the butcher cut the lamb shoulder into chops. Clean and trim the fat off the chops. Melt butter in skillet. Sauté the chops with seasonings until the chops are done. Add water and let cook on low fire for 10 minutes. Wash, clean, and chop the vegetables. Put them aside. Cook rice as in directions for chelo (see p. 65). When you come to step *6* of the directions for chelo, after putting half of the rice in the pot, arrange meat and some of the vegetables in alternating order until the top layer is covered with the rice. Cover and cook as directed for chelo. Delicious when served with yogurt.

Makes 4-5 servings.

 82 *In a Persian Kitchen*

Lubia Sabz Polo

Rice with String Beans

1 lb. round beef or stew meat, cut into 1/2" cubes	1/2 cup tomato sauce
2 tbsp. butter	1/2 cup water
1 medium onion (finely chopped)	2 1/2 cups rice
1/2 tsp. salt	1 1/2 tbsp. salt
1/4 tsp. pepper	2 qt. water
1/2 tsp. cinnamon	2 tbsp. salt
1 1/2 lb. string beans (cut into thirds)	1/2 cup butter

Melt butter in a 3-quart pot. Add meat, onions, and seasoning and sauté until meat is browned. Add water, tomato sauce, and string beans to the meat and let simmer for 30 minutes. Cook rice as in directions for chelo (see p. 65). When you come to step *6* of the directions for chelo, after putting half of the rice in the pot, arrange the meat and the string-bean mixture over the rice. Pour the rest of the rice over the meat mixture. Cook as directed for chelo. *Makes 4–5 servings.*

Sauces for Pilafs

Khoresh in Persian stands for a stewy type of sauce which is usually prepared with meat or fowl combined with fresh or dried vegetables, fresh or dried fruit, or sometimes nuts and cereals.

Persians almost always eat their rice with khoresh. Usually, a plate full of white fluffy rice is served topped with khoresh. When rice is served with khoresh it is referred to as "Chelo Khoresh."

Chelo Khoresh is a favorite of all the Persians. If you ever take a trip to Persia you will find this dish served at least once a day. No matter how many dishes a housewife prepares for lunch or dinner, there is always a Chelo Khoresh dish at the table. Since Chelo Khoresh is so popular, the Persian housewife tries to prepare it with various types of khoresh.

In the springtime, when fresh vegetables are available, the Persian housewife uses her ingenuity in combining such exotic vegetables as rhubarb, eggplants, spinach, mushrooms, and others with various kinds of meat or fowl. In summer, she takes advantage of the fresh fruit available in the market and creates the most delicately flavored sauce from fresh peaches, green plums, or sour cherries and combines it cleverly with chicken or meat. In the fall she creates the most exquisitely flavored sauce from quinces, tart apples, and pumpkins, combined with meat or fowl. As the winter season approaches and as the fresh vegetables and fruits become scarce, she makes the most of the nuts and the dried fruits available. She uses the seasoning techniques taught by her ancestors and produces khoresh using wild duck with pomegranates and walnuts or lamb and prunes seasoned with cinnamon.

Khoresh is a very easy sauce to prepare. The secret of a good khoresh lies in seasoning. If you acquire the right touch in seasoning you have achieved the right technique. Many of the khoreshes given in this chapter are very economical to prepare and do not require much time. They can be prepared a day or two in advance and do not lose their taste.

In this chapter I have tried to give you a very easy method to follow. Basically, most khoreshes are prepared the same way. The difference lies in seasoning and ingredients. So, if you master one, I am sure you can manage those that sound very hard and complicated to prepare.

Khoreshe Alu

Prune Sauce

My grandmother used to refer to Khoreshe Alu as *sardi*, or cold, and when a member of the family was not feeling well Grandmother would prepare this khoresh.

To an American palate the combination of meat and prunes might sound odd, but you must really try this khoresh in order to realize the delicate flavor that can be formed from meat, prunes, seasoning, and a touch of lemon.

Prune Sauce

2 tbsp. butter
1 lb. stew beef or round beef
    cut in 1" cubes
1 large onion (finely chopped)
1 tsp. salt
1/4 tsp. pepper

1/4 tsp. nutmeg
1/4 tsp. cinnamon
2 cups water
1 1/2 tbsp. lemon juice
20–25 dried prunes (soaked)

Melt the butter in a 2-quart pot. Add meat, onions, and seasoning. Sauté on medium fire. Add water and lemon juice to the meat and let simmer for about 35 minutes. 15 minutes before serving pour off the water from the prunes and add the prunes to the meat. Let simmer on a low fire for 15 minutes. Serve it with chelo. *Makes about 4 servings.*

Khoreshe Anar

Pomegranate Sauce

2 1/2–3 lb. fryer (cut up)
4 tbsp. shortening
1 tsp. salt
1/2 tsp. poultry seasoning
1/4 tsp. pepper
1/4 tsp. paprika
1 1/4 cups water

1 onion (finely chopped)
3 tbsp. butter
3/4 cup pomegranate seeds
15–20 dried apricots
3 tbsp. butter
1/4 cup lemon juice
1/2 cup sugar

Wash and prepare the chicken for frying. Sauté the chicken with seasoning in shortening until golden. Add water and let simmer on a low fire for 25–30 minutes. As an alternate method the chicken may be baked in a 350° oven for 45 minutes instead. Sauté the onions in butter until golden. Add pomegranates to the onions and sauté them a few more minutes. Wash the apricots a few times and sauté them in butter for 5 minutes. Add the sautéed onions and pomegranates and apricots to the chicken. Mix lemon juice and sugar and add it to the chicken and let simmer for about 20 minutes. If the sauce is thick add more water. Serve over chelo. *Makes 4–5 servings.*

Khoreshe Bagali

Lima Bean Sauce

3 tbsp. butter	2 *cups yogurt*
1 *lb. stew beef or round beef cut in*	1 *egg*
1" *cubes*	1 1/2 *tsp. curry powder*
1 *large onion (finely chopped)*	1 *tsp. salt*
1/2 *cup water*	1/2 *tsp. pepper*
1 *pkg. frozen baby lima beans*	

Melt butter in a skillet. Sauté the beef and the onions until golden brown. Add 1/2 cup of water and the lima beans and let simmer on a low fire for about 25 minutes or until meat is tender. Meanwhile, put the yogurt in a double boiler and add egg and seasoning. Add meat and the beans to the yogurt mixture. Cook in a double boiler on a low fire for about 20 minutes, stirring constantly to prevent yogurt from curdling. Serve over chelo. *Makes 4–6 servings.*

Khoreshe Bademjan

Eggplant Sauce

When I first came to the United States I was very surprised to learn that people knew very little about the very delicate vegetable, eggplant. If they had eaten it, it had been dipped in batter and fried, and those who had eaten eggplants prepared this way claimed that they didn't care much for it. And no wonder! There are many ways of preparing eggplant, and the Persian housewife knows how to prepare it in at least a hundred different ways.

I love eggplants, and you will be amazed to know how many of my friends I have taught to appreciate this delicious vegetable. In order to compile this book, as I have already mentioned, I tested all the recipes with my American friends, giving parties, inviting my American friends to dinners, or preparing meals at their homes whenever there was an opportunity to do so. A couple of times I prepared dinner for a

group of eight Harvard bachelors residing in Washington, D.C. They came from eight different states and some of them had never heard of eggplants or, if they had, they had eaten only fried eggplants. On one occasion I prepared Khoreshe Bâdem-jân for them. When I described the ingredients that went into this sauce, they looked aghast and couldn't believe that it could taste good, but since they had previously tasted some of my cooking, they let me cook this sauce for them. I will never forget their astonishment when they tasted chelo and Khoreshe Bâdemjân. In a very short time the dishes were cleaned and not a morsel was left.

The secret of preparing eggplant well and preserving its delicate flavor lies in the removing of its bitterness, as the following recipe will illustrate.

2 *medium eggplants*	1/2 *tsp. pepper*
2 *tbsp. salt*	1/4 *tsp. nutmeg*
2 *tbsp. butter*	6 *tbsp. shortening*
1 *lb. stew beef or round beef cut in*	1 1/4 *cups tomato sauce*
1″ *cubes*	1 3/4 *cups water*
1 *medium onion (finely chopped)*	3–4 *tbsp. lemon juice*
1 *tsp. salt*	1 *large tomato (optional)*
1/2 *tsp. cinnamon*	

Cut the unpeeled eggplants lengthwise into 1″ slices. Wash, sprinkle with salt, and let stand for about 20 minutes. (This takes away the bitterness of the eggplants.) Melt the butter in a 3-quart saucepan. Add meat, onions, and seasoning and sauté. Add tomato sauce, water, and lemon juice to the meat and let simmer for about 35 minutes on a low fire. Wash the salt off the eggplants and dry them with a paper towel. Melt the shortening and sauté the eggplants separately. 15 minutes before serving, add the eggplants and quartered tomatoes to the meat and let simmer. Serve this sauce over chelo. This recipe can be made without the tomato sauce and tomatoes. Just increase the amount of water and lemon juice. You can substitute chicken for meat. It is very delicious with chicken, and chicken cooked in such a sauce acquires a very delicate flavor.

Makes 5–6 servings.

Khoreshe Esfanaj

Spinach Sauce

1/4 cup black-eyed peas	1/2 tsp. cinnamon
1 1/2 cups water	1/4 tsp. nutmeg
4 tbsp. shortening	3 tbsp. shortening
1 lb. stew beef or round beef cut in 1" cubes	1 lb. fresh spinach
1 large onion (finely chopped)	1 cup fresh parsley
1 tsp. salt	2 cups water
1/2 tsp. pepper	juice of a small lemon

Cook the black-eyed peas in 1 1/2 cups water on a medium fire for about 20 minutes. Melt shortening in a 2-quart pot. Add meat, onions, and seasoning and sauté until the meat is browned. Wash the spinach and parsley thoroughly and chop. Melt shortening in a frying pan and sauté the vegetables for 10 minutes. Add 2 cups of water and lemon juice to the meat and let simmer on a low fire for about 35 minutes. 20 minutes before serving add the sautéed vegetables to the meat and let simmer for 20 minutes or a little more. Serve with chelo.

Makes 4–5 servings.

Khoreshe Beh

Quince Sauce

Beh, or quince, is a very popular fruit back home in Persia. I remember when the months of October and November would approach, Mother used to make her famous Khoreshe Beh, and our family always looked forward to this delicious sauce during these months when quinces were in season.

In America quince is rarely used. It is only known in jams and jellies, and these are not very popular preserves. Persians, however, know many ways to prepare quince. Stuffed quince or quince cooked with meat in a khoresh is a very delicate and worthwhile dish.

2 *large quinces*	1/2 *tsp. pepper*
3 *tbsp. butter*	1/2 *tsp. cinnamon*
4 *tbsp. shortening*	1/4 *tsp. nutmeg*
1 *lb. stew beef or round beef cut in*	2 *cups water*
1″ *cubes*	3 *tbsp. lemon juice*
1 *large onion (finely chopped)*	2 *tsp. sugar*
1 *tsp. salt*	1/3 *cup yellow split peas*

Wash, core, and cut the quinces in slices as for apple pie. Sauté the sliced quinces in butter. Melt shortening in a 2-quart pot. Add meat, onions, and seasoning and sauté on a medium fire until the meat is browned. Add water, lemon juice, and sugar to meat and let simmer for 30 minutes on a low fire. 25 minutes before serving add split peas and continue cooking. About 15 minutes before serving add sautéed quince to the meat mixture and let simmer on a low fire for 15 minutes. Serve with chelo. *Makes 4–5 servings.*

Khoreshe Fesenjan

Chicken with Pomegranate Sauce

As long as I can remember Khoreshe Fesenjân has been my favorite dish. How well I recall the first time I tasted this exotic khoresh. It was prepared by my grandmother, who in her own right was famous for the preparation of this particular sauce. Although I was very young, I still can remember the sensation I received from eating Fesenjân. The rich, subtle, and extraordinary taste of Fesenjân left me with a satisfaction that I had never before experienced.

I recall so vividly the days when Fesenjân was served for lunch. On those days every member of my family would come home early in order not to miss their portion.

I always connect Fesenjân with the winter season. As I have already said, certain khoreshes in Persia are seasonal. Fesenjân was definitely a winter dish in our house. There were always many stories as to why Fesenjân shouldn't be served in other seasons. Grandmother believed that in order to acquire the real exotic taste of Fesenjân one should prepare it with wild duck or pheasant and use fresh pomegranate juice. The months of November and December are the hunting months for wild duck on the Caspian Sea shores, and we always used to receive wild ducks from my relatives who lived there.

Grandmother used to say, "Fesenjân is hot, therefore one shouldn't eat it in summer time." Persians divide food into two categories; they call some *sardi* and others *garmi*. Sardi means cold and garmi means warm. In other words, some foods should be eaten in summer time because they have a cooling effect and others should be eaten in winter because they have a warming effect.

Anyway, whether Fesenjân is garmi or sardi I think that you should try it once and decide for yourself.

2 1/2–3 *lb. fryer (cut up)*	2 *cups walnuts (finely chopped)*
5 *tbsp. shortening*	3 1/2 *cups water*
1/2 *tsp. poultry seasoning*	1 *tsp. salt*
1 *tsp. salt*	1/2 *tsp. cinnamon*
1/2 *tsp. pepper*	2 *tbsp. lemon juice*
1 *large onion (finely chopped)*	1 *cup fresh pomegranate juice*
3 *tbsp. butter*	or 2–3 *tbsp. syrup (see p. 170)*
2 *tbsp. tomato sauce*	1 *tbsp. sugar*

Wash and prepare the chicken for frying. Sauté the chicken with seasoning in shortening until light brown on all sides. As an alternate method the chicken may be baked in a 350°

oven for 45 minutes. Put aside. Sauté the onions in 3 tablespoons butter until golden brown. Add tomato sauce and sauté for a few minutes. Add walnuts to the sautéed onions and sauté over a medium fire for about 5 minutes. Stir constantly and be careful not to burn the walnuts. Add water, seasoning, lemon juice, and pomegranate syrup. Cover and let cook on a low fire for about 35 minutes. Taste the sauce and if you find it a little sour add sugar. Arrange the sautéed chicken in this sauce. Cover and let simmer for 20–25 minutes. Serve with chelo.

Makes 5–6 servings.

[Note] Wild duck or beef can be used as easily. If wild duck is used, follow the directions for chicken. If beef is used, cut it up in 1″ cubes and don't use poultry seasoning. Also, if frozen orange juice is available, substitute 2 tablespoons lemon juice and 1 tablespoon sugar with 1 small can of frozen orange juice. Add the orange juice when the seasoning and the pomegranate sauce are added.

Khoreshe Geimeh

Meat and Yellow Split Pea Sauce

There are many old wives' tales as to how and why this khoresh has become so popular with the Persian housewife. As I have already mentioned in the Introduction, Persians have been known for their hospitality for many centuries. I am again

reminded of the famous Persian saying: *Mehman Hediyeh Khodâst,* "A guest is God's gift." Because a Persian house is always open to an unexpected guest, a Persian man would never hesitate to bring four or five guests for lunch without informing his wife in advance. The Persian housewife has solved this problem in her own way. She knows that it isn't right for her to tell her husband or her son that she prefers to know beforehand whom he is bringing for lunch or dinner. She knows that this is a national custom and that she is not going to be able to train her family to do otherwise. She has solved this problem by learning how to keep the necessary food on hand.

She has learned from her mother and grandmother how to cook and preserve meat in earthen jugs and how to keep it so that it will not spoil. This method is known as *geimeh.*

Basically, you recall, Persian khoresh is made of meat that has been cut in 1″ or 1/2″ cubes and sautéed in butter with seasoning. This type of cutting of the meat in Persian is known as geimeh. When meat is plentiful and good, the Persian housewife sautées and seasons the meat and stores it in earthen jugs for use during the long winter months, when she is not able to obtain fresh meat. When unexpected guests arrive, she goes to her *anbâr*, or pantry, and opens up the jug containing geimeh.

Geimeh can be mixed with fresh or dry vegetables or various sorts of peas. The original Khoresh Geimeh is a combination of meat and yellow split peas. Of course, each family has its own way of varying it. Some like to add sautéed potatoes and others prefer to vary the taste by adding dried prunes. It is a very easy khoresh to prepare and also a very economical and delicious one.

Meat and Yellow Split Pea Sauce

4 tbsp. shortening
1 lb. stew beef or round beef cut in
   1/2" cubes
1 large onion (finely chopped)
1 tsp. salt
1/2 tsp. pepper
1/2 tsp. cinnamon

1/4 tsp. nutmeg
1/4 tsp. turmerick
juice of small lime or lemon
2 1/2 cups water
1/4 cup yellow split peas
1 large potato
3 tbsp. shortening

Melt shortening in a 2-quart pot. Add meat, onions, and seasoning and sauté until the meat is browned. Add lime juice and water to the meat and let simmer for about 30 minutes. Add split peas and let simmer for another 35 minutes or until the peas are done. Peel the potatoes and dice and fry them in shortening. Add fried potatoes to the meat sauce 10 minutes before serving. Serve with chelo. *Makes 4–5 servings.*

Khoreshe Garch

Mushroom Sauce

3 tbsp. butter
1–1 1/2 lb. lamb or beef cut in 1"
   cubes
1 medium onion (finely chopped)
1 tsp. salt
1/2 tsp. pepper
1/2 tsp. cinnamon

1 1/2 cups water
3 tbsp. lemon juice
1 lb. fresh mushrooms
2 tbsp. butter
2 egg yolks
2 tbsp. lemon juice

Melt butter in a skillet and sauté the meat, onions, and seasoning until browned. Add water and lemon juice and let meat simmer over a low fire for about 30 minutes until the meat is tender. Wash, clean, and chop the mushrooms. Sauté them in butter. Add the sautéed mushrooms to the meat about 15 minutes before serving. Beat 2 egg yolks with lemon juice. Add them to the meat sauce after you remove the skillet from the fire and when you are ready to serve. Serve with chelo. If desired, add 2 or 3 tablespoons of sherry wine when you add the mushrooms. *Makes 4-5 servings.*

Khoreshe Gormeh Sabzi

Green Vegetable Sauce

Khoreshe Gormeh Sabzi is a very popular khoresh with all the Persians. Whether poor or rich, every Persian housewife serves this khoresh to her family at least once a week.

I believe that the popularity of this khoresh comes from the fact that it really isn't a seasonal sauce. Although the main ingredients of this khoresh are vegetables and should really be prepared when fresh vegetables are in season, the Persian housewife can use instead the dried vegetables which she always has on hand.

A good Persian housewife, or, as we say in Persian, a

Khânome Khânehdâr, always has dried vegetables stored away in her *anbâr*, or pantry. Therefore, when the winter season approaches, she is able to surprise her family with this khoresh.

Khoreshe Gormeh Sabzi is economical and easy to prepare and delicious served over chelo.

Green Vegetable Sauce

1/3 *cup black-eyed peas*
1 1/2 *cups water*
4 *tbsp. shortening*
1 *lb. stew beef or round beef cut in*
   1" *cubes*
1 *medium onion (finely chopped)*
1 *tsp. salt*
1/2 *tsp. pepper*
1/2 *tsp. cinnamon*

1/4 *tsp. nutmeg*
4 *tbsp. shortening*
1 *cup chopped green onions*
1 *cup leek (chopped)*
1 *cup spinach (chopped)*
1 *cup parsley (chopped)*
2 *cups water*
3 *tbsp. lemon juice*

Cook peas in 1 1/2 cups water on a medium fire for about 20 minutes. Melt shortening in 2-quart pot. Add meat, onions, and seasoning and sauté until the meat is browned. Meanwhile, melt 4 tablespoons shortening in a frying pan and add chopped green onions, leek, spinach, and parsley and sauté for 10 minutes. Add 2 cups of water and lemon juice to the meat, cover, and let simmer for about 30 minutes. When meat is tender, add cooked peas and vegetables 15–20 minutes before serving. Serve with chelo. *Makes 4–5 servings.*

"He who believeth in one God and in a future life, let him honor his guest."
MOHAMMAD

Khoreshe Mast va Kari

Yogurt and Curry Sauce

I have already spoken about yogurt and the variety of dishes which a Persian housewife can prepare with it. In this khoresh, again, the Persian housewife uses her ingenuity in combining the right amount of yogurt and curry powder and creates a khoresh that is unique in taste.

I was fortunate enough to acquire this particular recipe from a private collection and have served it many times to my American friends, who like the exotic combination of yogurt and curry.

2 1/2–3 *lb. stewing chicken (cut up)*	1 *large onion (finely chopped)*
2 1/2 *cups water*	1 *tsp. salt*
1 *tsp. salt*	1/2 *tsp. pepper*
1/2 *tsp. pepper*	1/2 *tsp. allspice*
2 *stalks celery*	1 *tsp. curry powder*
1 *qt. yogurt (4 cups)*	1 *tbsp. flour*
2 *eggs*	1/2 *cube butter*

Place the chicken in kettle with seasoning and water. Cover and simmer covered for about 1 hour or until a fork can be easily inserted in leg. Cool chicken and broth. Store the broth in refrigerator for soup or other uses. Remove skin and bones, then cut meat in strips. Put yogurt in a double boiler and add eggs, chopped onions, and seasoning. Mix well. Add flour gradually. Put the double boiler on a low fire and stir mixture constantly for about 10 minutes until it thickens. Be careful not to curdle the yogurt. Add the chicken and the butter to the yogurt mixture and let it cook for another 5 minutes over a low fire. This sauce can be made with lamb or stew meat. Serve with chelo. *Makes 4–5 servings.*

Khoreshe Kadu

Squash Sauce

4–5 *medium squash (zucchini)*	1/2 *tsp. cinnamon*
2 *tbsp. salt*	1/4 *tsp. pepper*
3 *tbsp. shortening*	1/8 *tsp. nutmeg*
1 *lb. stew beef or round beef cut in*	6 *tbsp. shortening*
1″ *cubes*	1–2 *cups water*
1 *tsp. salt*	3 *tbsp. lemon juice*

Cut the squash lengthwise into 1″ strips. Wash and sprinkle with salt. Let them stand for 20 minutes. (This process takes away the bitterness of the squash.) Melt the shortening in a 2-quart saucepan. Add meat, onions, and seasoning and sauté. Wash the salt off the squash and dry with a paper towel. Melt 6 tablespoons of shortening and sauté the squash separately. Now add water and lemon juice to the meat and let it simmer for about 30 minutes on a low fire. 15 minutes before serving, add the squash and let simmer. Serve with chelo.

Makes 4–5 servings.

Khoreshe Karafs

Celery Sauce

I think Khoreshe Karafs should appeal to the young American housewife. It is indeed a very economical dish and also easy to prepare. It doesn't require much time and can easily be prepared in advance and warmed up before serving. The seasoning and the right amount of lemon juice added to this khoresh make it a wonderful sauce over chelo.

4 *tbsp. butter*
1 *lb. stew beef or round beef cut in*
   1″ *cubes*
1 *large onion (finely chopped)*
1/2 *tsp. pepper*
1 *tsp. salt*
1 *tsp. cinnamon*

1/4 *tsp. nutmeg*
2 *cups water*
4 *tbsp. butter*
4 *cups diced celery*
1 *cup chopped parsley*
3 *tbsp. lemon juice*

Melt butter in a 2-quart pot. Add meat, onions, and seasoning and sauté until the meat is browned. Add water to the meat, cover, and let cook for about 30 minutes or until the meat is tender. Melt 4 tablespoons butter in a skillet, add celery and parsley, and sauté it for 10 minutes. Add the sautéed vegetables and lemon juice to the meat and let simmer for another 15 minutes. Serve with chelo. *Makes 4–5 servings.*

Khoreshe Sak

Spinach and Orange Sauce

I am sure that the combination of spinach and orange, flavored with garlic, sounds very strange to the American palate. But Khoreshe Sak is one of the native dishes of the Mazandaran area, whose people are noted for deft usage of citrus fruits in their dishes. Mazandaran is one of the few areas where rice is commonly eaten three times a day.

In order to vary the rice dishes, the Mazandarani housewife uses much imagination in combining meat with the citrus fruits that are plentiful along the Caspian Sea shores.

1 *lb. ground beef*	1 *cup water*
1 *medium onion (grated)*	1 *cup orange juice*
1/2 *tsp. salt*	1/4 *cup lemon juice*
1/4 *tsp. pepper*	1 *tbsp. flour*
1/4 *tsp. cinnamon*	1 *tsp. salt*
3 *tbsp. butter*	1 *clove garlic (chopped)*
1 *lb. fresh spinach (chopped)*	2 *tbsp. butter*
1 *cup parsley (chopped)*	

Put the meat in a large bowl. Add onions and seasoning and mix well. Form meat balls the size of walnuts. Melt butter in a skillet and sauté the meat balls for 10 minutes until the meat

 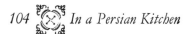

is brown. Wash the spinach thoroughly. Dry and chop very finely. Wash, dry, and chop parsley. Melt shortening in a skillet and sauté the vegetables for 10 minutes. Mix the meat and the vegetables together, add water, and let simmer on a low fire for about 15 minutes. Mix orange juice, lemon juice, and flour together. Add to the meat and vegetable mixture. Add salt if needed. Let simmer for another 20 minutes. Chop garlic finely and sauté it in butter and add it to the meat and vegetable mixture about 10 minutes before serving. Serve with chelo.

Makes 4–5 servings.

Khoreshe Holu

Peach Sauce

Many historians believe that peaches originally came to Europe from China through Persia and that they hence acquired their name from the name of the land itself. If we examine the words for peach in a few languages we will see that they are all derived from the same basic root. In French we call this delicate fruit *pêche;* in Russian it is *persik;* in Italian, *pesca;* and in German it is written *Pfirsich.*

Peaches originally were introduced to the Western World

from ancient Persia. The best-flavored peaches are grown in the northeastern part of Persia, known as Khorâsân. Persian poets have written many sonnets about this fruit, and peach dishes have always been favorites of all Persians.

Naturally Persians haven't been satisfied with preparing peaches in an ordinary way. Through years of practice they have created many different peach dishes, producing some unusual and successful results.

One of the common uses of peaches is in combination with fowl or meat, flavored with lemon and sugar. It might again sound very odd to you, but you must try it to appreciate the true flavor of Khoreshe Holu.

Peach Sauce

4 tbsp. shortening	2 tbsp. butter
1 lb. meat lamb or stew beef in 1" cubes or 2 1/2–3 lb. chicken (cut up)	1 medium onion (finely chopped)
	1 tbsp. lemon juice
	4 large peaches (not ripe)
1 tsp. salt	2 tbsp. butter
1/2 tsp. pepper	1/4 cup lime and lemon juice (mixed)
1/4 tsp. paprika	1/2 cup sugar
1/2 tsp. poultry seasoning	3/4 cup water
1 1/4 cups water	

Melt shortening in a large frying pan and sauté the meat or chicken with the seasonings until browned. Add water and let simmer on a low fire for about 25 minutes. Melt 2 tablespoons butter in another frying pan and sauté the onions until golden. Remove, add one tablespoon of lemon juice, and let stand. Wash the peaches well to remove the fuzz. Cut them in half and remove the seeds. Then slice them (as for apple pie). Melt butter in a frying pan and sauté the peaches until they are golden. Add the onions to the meat or chicken and arrange the peaches over the meat. Mix lime and lemon juice and sugar and add it to the meat or chicken mixture. Then add 3/4 of a cup of water, cover, and let simmer on a low fire for 20 minutes. Use cinnamon instead of poultry seasoning if meat is used. Serve with chelo.   *Makes 4–5 servings.*

Khoreshe Portagal

Orange Sauce

2 1/2–3 *lb. fryer (cut up)*
4–5 *tbsp. shortening*
1/2 *tsp. poultry seasoning*
1 *tsp. salt*
1/2 *tsp. pepper*
1/4 *tsp. paprika*
1 1/4 *cups water*

1 *large onion (finely chopped)*
3 *tbsp. butter*
1 *tbsp. lemon juice*
4–5 *oranges (peeled and segmented)*
1/4 *cup vinegar*
1/2 *cup sugar*

Wash and prepare the chicken for frying. Sauté the chicken with seasoning in shortening until golden. Add water and let simmer on a low fire for 25–30 minutes. Sauté the onions in shortening until golden, add lemon juice, and let stand. Peel oranges and segment them. Put them in a pan. Mix vinegar and sugar and add it to the oranges and let simmer on a low fire for 15 minutes. Arrange sautéed oranges and onions on the chicken. Add the sweet-and-sour sauce from the orange to the chicken. If you find this sauce sour, add sugar to taste. Let simmer for 15 minutes on a low fire. Serve with chelo.

Makes 4–5 servings.

Kukuye Sib

Apple and Meat Sauce

I can say with assurance that Persians know better than anyone else how to combine fruits with meat and other ingredients. Khoreshe Sib is one of these clever combinations which demonstrates the artistic ingenuity of the Persian housewife. One of my favorite sauces, Khoreshe Sib is an extremely easy and economical dish to prepare. I have prepared this dish many times and its novel flavor has delighted my American friends.

4 *tbsp. butter*	1/2 *tsp. pepper*
1 *large onion (finely chopped).*	1/2 *tsp. cinnamon*
1 *tbsp. lemon juice*	2 *cups water*
1 *lb. stew or round beef cut in 1"*	1 *tsp. lemon juice*
cubes	4–5 *tart apples*
1 *tsp. salt*	3 *tbsp. butter*

Melt butter in a 2-quart pot. Sauté onions until golden. Remove onions and add lemon juice and set aside. Sauté the meat with seasoning until the meat is browned. Add water and

 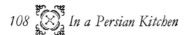

lemon juice and let simmer on a low fire for about 30 minutes or until meat is done. Wash, core, and slice apples as for apple pie. Melt butter in a skillet and sauté the apples in the butter for 5 minutes. 5–10 minutes before serving, add onions to the meat and arrange the sautéed apples around the meat and let simmer on a very low fire for 5 minutes. Serve with chelo.

Makes 4–5 servings.

Khoreshe Lubia Sabz

String Bean Sauce

4 *tbsp. butter*	1/4 *tsp. nutmeg*
1 *lb. stew beef or round beef cut in*	2 *cups water*
1" *cubes*	1 *lb. string beans*
1 *large onion (finely chopped)*	1 *tsp. baking soda*
1 *tsp. salt*	3 *tbsp. butter*
1/2 *tsp. pepper*	3–4 *tbsp. lemon juice*
1/2 *tsp. cinnamon*	

Melt butter in a 2-quart pan. Sauté the onions and put them aside. Sauté the meat with seasoning until the meat is browned. Add onions and water and let simmer on a low fire for about 30 minutes. Wash and cut the string beans as for shoestring potatoes. Boil them in water and soda (use soda if you wish to retain their bright green color) for about 10 minutes. Drain and sauté the beans in butter about 10 minutes. Add the beans and lemon juice to the meat and let it simmer for 25 minutes on a low fire until the meat is done. If more seasoning or lemon juice is needed, add to taste. Serve with chelo.

Makes 4–5 servings.

Khoreshe Rivâs

Rhubarb Sauce

I remember Grandmother referring to Khoreshe Rivâs, as *sardi*, or cold. Khoreshe Rivâs was always served in our house when children as well as adults were suffering from indigestion. Grandmother, who had a great knowledge of medicine, always had a natural remedy for all ailments. In her practice of medicine she cured her patients with remedies made of natural herbs and in her culinary art she used her ingenuity to keep us on a proper diet which was healthy and yet exquisitely prepared.

I have eaten rhubarb in this country in many forms. I think that Americans make excellent desserts out of rhubarb, but I have rarely tasted rhubarb combined with meat and seasoning. Khoreshe Rivâs is a very refreshing sauce when served over chelo. Besides having a medicinal value this sauce is unique in taste and economical and easy to prepare.

4 tbsp. butter
1 lb. stew or round beef cut in 1"
  cubes
1 large onion (finely chopped)
1 tsp. salt
1/2 tsp. pepper

1/2 tsp. cinnamon
1/4 tsp. nutmeg
1 cup parsley (chopped)
2 cups water
1 lb. rhubarb

Melt butter in a 2-quart pot. Add meat, onions, and seasoning and sauté until meat is browned. Add chopped parsley and sauté a few minutes more. Add water to the meat, cover, and let simmer for about 40 minutes on a low fire or until the meat is tender. String the rhubarb and cut it in 3" slices. Add rhubarb to the meat sauce 5 minutes before serving and let simmer. Serve with chelo. *Makes 4–5 servings.*

"*Patience is a bitter cup which the strong alone can drink.*"
ARAB WISDOM

Egg Casserole
Dishes

Kuku is a type of dish usually made of vegetables and eggs. It can also be made of meat and chicken and eggs. (Eggs are the basis for these casserole dishes because they serve as the binding element.) This is a very popular dish with the Persian housewife for it can be served cold as well as warm and also can be prepared in advance. Kuku dishes make a very easy and attractive main course. In Persia, however, this dish isn't served as a main course. In our house this dish was always served as a side dish or appetizer. Since this dish tastes excellent cold, it is very often used as a picnic food. We take it along when we have picnics on Fridays, the Moslem Sabbath day.

I think that this dish should have special appeal to the American housewife because it uses the same principle as American casserole dishes.

Kukuye Bâdemjan

Eggplant Casserole

I have already mentioned the popularity of bâdemjân or eggplants among the Persians. Kukuye Bâdemjân, a favorite of mine, is a dish which brings out the real taste of the eggplants. In Persia, this dish is often served as an appetizer; however, it makes a very satisfactory luncheon or light dinner.

4 *medium eggplants*	3 *tbsp. lemon juice*
1/3 *cup shortening*	4 *egg whites*
2 *tsp. salt*	4 *egg yolks*
1 *tsp. pepper*	2 *tbsp. butter*
1/2 *tsp. garlic*	

Peel the eggplants. Cut them lengthwise and wash them. Drain the water well and sauté them in shortening until golden brown. Let cool. Put the eggplants in a bowl and mash them well. Add seasoning and lemon juice and mix well. Beat the egg whites well, until foamy. Fold in the egg yolks. Fold this mixture into the mashed eggplants. Melt butter in a 9″ casserole or cake pan. Pour the eggplant mixture in the pan and bake it in a 350° oven for about 45 minutes or until done. Serve it topped with yogurt. As a variation, grate some sharp cheese and add to the eggplant mixture before pouring it into the pan.

Makes 4 servings.

Kukuye Sabzi

Vegetable Casserole

Kukuye Sabzi is one of Mother's special recipes which I have always enjoyed. Kukuye Sabzi is a favorite of all Persians. No matter how many dishes a Persian housewife prepares when she entertains for dinner she will be sure to have Kukuye Sabzi at the table.

This dish should appeal to the housewife wherever, as in America, fresh vegetables are plentiful and can be obtained at all seasons for reasonable prices.

Kukuye Sabzi is a well-balanced meal in itself. It contains all the necessary vitamins and tastes superb when served cold. Try this dish for a cocktail party and surprise your guests.

2 *cups leek (finely chopped)*	1 1/4 *tsp. salt*
1 *cup lettuce (finely chopped)*	1/2 *tsp. pepper*
1 *cup parsley (finely chopped)*	1/3 *cup chopped walnuts*
2 *cups spinach (finely chopped)*	8 *eggs*
1 *cup green onions (finely chopped)*	1/3 *cup butter*
1 1/2 *tbsp. flour*	

Put all the chopped vegetables in a bowl. Add flour, salt, and pepper and mix well. Add walnuts and mix. Beat the eggs well and add them to the vegetables. Melt the butter in a 9″ cake pan and pour the vegetables in the pan. Cook in 325°

preheated oven for an hour or until the top is crisp and brown. Serve with yogurt.   *Makes 4-5 servings.*

Kukuye Bademjan va Kadu

Eggplant and Squash Casserole

5 *tbsp. shortening*	1/2 *tsp. salt*
1 *medium onion (chopped)*	1/2 *tsp. pepper*
2 *tbsp. lemon juice*	1/2 *tsp. cinnamon*
2 *eggplants*	1/4 *tsp. paprika*
4 *squashes*	2 *tbsp. lemon juice*
5 *eggs*	

Sauté the onions in the shortening and put aside. Add lemon juice and let the onions stay for a while. Cut the eggplants lengthwise in quarters, then cut them into 2″ thicknesses. Peel the squash and dice them. Wash and salt the eggplants and the squash and let stand for 15 minutes. Wash off the salt and sauté the eggplants and the squash in shortening until they are golden brown. Beat the eggs well, add the sautéed onions to the eggs, and mix well. Add seasoning and lemon juice to the sautéed eggplants and squash. Pour the eggs over the eggplants and squash. Cover and let cook over a medium fire for about 20 minutes. Serve topped with yogurt.   *Makes 4 servings.*

Kukuye Gusht

Meat Casserole

3 *tbsp. butter*	1 1/4 *tsp. salt*
1 *lb. ground beef*	1 *tsp. curry powder*
1 *large onion (finely chopped)*	1/4 *tsp. cinnamon*
1 *cup spinach (chopped)*	1/4 *tsp. pepper*
1/2 *cup leek or green onions (chopped)*	5 *eggs*

Melt the butter in a skillet. Sauté the meat and the onions for 15 minutes. Clean, wash, and chop the spinach, parsley, and leek. Add chopped vegetables to the meat. Add seasoning and mix well. Beat eggs slightly and add them to the meat and vegetable mixture. Mix well. Grease the bottom of a 9″ pie pan. Pour mixture in the pan and cook in 325° preheated oven for about 30 minutes. Serve with yogurt.   *Makes 4 servings.*

Kukuye Sib Zamina va Gojeh Farangi

Potato and Tomato Casserole

Kukuye Sib Zamini va Gojeh Farangi always reminds me of my first cooking experience. One hot summer, when I was

 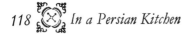

in Tehran, my family had left for our country house in Shemirân and had taken along the cook. My father and I were the only ones left at home. My father, like any old-fashioned Persian man, was in the habit of coming home for lunch and eating a home-cooked meal. Since I was just learning how to cook and had never prepared a meal without my mother's or the cook's help, I decided to surprise my father and prepare his lunch. The meal I cooked for him was Kukuye Sib Zamini va Gojeh Farangi. I shall never forget the surprised and pleased look on his face. He was very proud that his youngest daughter could prepare a meal alone.

This kuku is really a summer dish, when red ripe tomatoes and new potatoes are in season in Persia. We always serve this dish with Nâneh Lavâsh (the very thin Persian bread).

4 *tbsp. butter*	1/2 *tsp. salt*
1 *large onion (finely chopped)*	1/4 *tsp. pepper*
2 *tbsp. lemon juice*	4 *eggs*
1 *large potato*	1/4 *tsp. salt*
2 *large tomatoes (sliced)*	1/4 *tsp. cinnamon*

Melt shortening in a skillet and sauté the onions until they are golden. Remove them from the grease and add lemon juice and let stand. Wash, pare, and slice the potatoes 1/4″ thick. Then wash them well in cold water. Fry the potatoes in the same skillet in which the onions were sautéed. Fry them until they are golden. Arrange tomatoes over the potatoes and add onions which have been soaked in lemon juice. Add seasoning. Cover and let simmer for 10 minutes on a low fire.

Beat the eggs with seasoning. Pour the eggs over the potatoes and the rest. Cover and let cook on a low fire for another 10 minutes. *Makes 4 servings.*

Kukuye Jujeh

Chicken Casserole

5 *tbsp. shortening*
2 *large onions (finely chopped)*
3 *tbsp. lemon juice*
1 *small fryer (cut up)*
1 *tsp. poultry seasoning*
1 *tsp. salt*
1/2 *tsp. pepper*

1 *cup water*
2 *tbsp. lemon juice*
8 *eggs*
1/2 *tsp. salt*
1/4 *tsp. pepper*
1/4 *tsp. cinnamon*

Melt shortening in a large skillet and sauté the onions until they are golden. Remove the onions from the skillet, add lemon juice, and put them aside. Clean and wash the fryer and sauté the pieces in the same skillet, adding seasoning. When all the chicken parts are browned, add 1 cup of water and 2 tablespoons lemon juice and let simmer on a low fire for 25 minutes or until all the water is gone. Beat the eggs with seasoning. Mix the onions with the beaten eggs and pour them over the chicken. Put the chicken in a 350° oven and let it cook for 20 minutes. This dish can also be made with leftover chicken and turkey. *Makes 5–6 servings.*

Kukuye Lubia Sabz

String Bean Casserole

1 lb. string beans
3 cups water
2 tbsp. salt
3 tbsp. butter
2 large onions (finely chopped)
1 lb. ground beef

1 1/2 tsp. salt
1/2 tsp. pepper
1/2 tsp. nutmeg
1 tsp. sugar
5–6 eggs
1 tbsp. lemon juice

Clean, wash, and cut the string beans in half. Boil them in 3 cups of water and 2 tablespoons of salt for 25 minutes or until tender. Sauté the onions and the meat in butter for 20 minutes. Drain the string beans and add to the meat mixture. Let cook slightly. Add half of the spices and sugar to the meat and the string beans. Beat the eggs slightly and add the rest of the spices and the sugar to the eggs. Mix well. Pour the beaten eggs over the meat and string bean mixture, add lemon, and mix well. Grease the bottom of a 10″ pie pan. Pour the mixture in the pan and cook in 325° preheated oven for about 45 minutes. *Makes 4–5 servings.*

Meat and Fowl

Chelo Kabab

Rice with Broiled Lamb

Chelo Kabâb is the queen of all kabâbs and is a specialty of Persia. I am sure most of you know what Shish Kabâb is and I am certain that many of you have tried it either in Middle Eastern restaurants or have made it yourselves at home. I am also sure that you have never tasted Chelo Kabâb unless you have visited Persia.

Chelo Kabâb is derived from two words: *chelo*, meaning cooked rice, and *kabâb*, meaning broiled meat or fowl. The best Chelo Kabâb is served at the Shamshiri restaurant in the Tehran Bazaar. Whether it is the secret of the owner of this restaurant, I don't know. I do know that those Americans who have visited Tehran and have tried this dish at the bazaar have never forgotten it and always discuss it when they meet with their Persian friends in this country.

To prepare the real Tehran Chelo Kabâb one should use filet of lamb. But, since that part of the lamb is hard to obtain in this country, leg of lamb or sometimes shoulder of lamb are good substitutes. The secret of good Chelo Kabâb is in the marination of the meat. The meat should be properly marinated in onion juice and sometimes in yogurt for a day or two.

There is an old Persian tradition as to how one should eat Chelo Kabâb. The proper way of serving Chelo Kabâb is to put plenty of chelo (see p. 65) in a plate, make a small hole in the center of it, and put egg yolk in it, then plenty of butter, the broiled Kabâb, and a teaspoon or two of sumac over it. Mix these ingredients well and start eating. I am sure that this description and this combination sounds very odd, but it is extremely delicious and quite different in taste.

Rice with Broiled Lamb

4–4 1/2 *lb. leg of lamb*
4 *tbsp. onion juice*
   or 1 *large onion grated*

1 *tsp. saffron (see p. 170)*
salt and pepper to taste
1–2 *tsp. sumac (see p. 170)*

Clean the lamb. Cut off excess fat. Cut the meat lengthwise into strips 1 1/2″ thick and 5″ long. Marinate this meat in grated onion and saffron. (This marinating process will make the meat very tasty and tender.) Cover the meat with wax paper and let it remain overnight in the frigidaire to marinate. When ready to cook, season it with salt and pepper to taste and broil it. Using a charcoal broiler will give better results. Serve this kabâb with chelo, plenty of butter, an egg yolk, and sumac.

Makes 6–7 servings.

Shish Kababe

Broiled Lamb on the Skewer

Shish Kabâb, originally takes its name from the Turkish language, *shish*, meaning "skewer," and *kabâb*, meaning "broiled." Every American housewife has heard of Shish Kabâb, and I have read many recipes in American cookbooks and magazines about its preparation.

In this book I will give you my own recipe for Shish Kabâb, which is very simple and very delicious. Personally, I believe that the secret of good Shish Kabâb is in marinating the meat. Of course there are many different opinions as to how one should prepare Shish Kabâb or even how one should marinate it. I have always marinated it in vinegar, onions, and oregano overnight and have served it broiled with broiled green peppers, onions, and tomatoes. I also believe that for best results Shish Kabâb should be broiled on charcoal.

4–5 *lb. leg of lamb*	4 *green peppers (2″ squares)*
2 *medium onions (grated)*	8 *very small sweet onions*
1 *tbsp. oregano*	6 *large tomatoes (quartered)*
2/3 *cup vinegar*	*salt and pepper to taste*

Clean the lamb. Cut off excess fat. Cut the meat in 2″ cubes. Marinate this meat in vinegar and grated onions and oregano. Cover the meat with wax paper and let it remain overnight in the frigidaire to marinate.

When ready to cook, season well with salt and pepper and put one slice of meat, green pepper, onion, and tomato on a skewer. Repeat this until skewer is full. There should be 4–5 pieces of each on the skewer. Broil this on the charcoal broiler.

Shish Kabâb is very often served with chelo or with French bread. If served with French bread, slice the bread lengthwise and as the kabâb becomes ready put the skewer in between the sliced bread and squeeze it slightly. Toast the bread over the charcoal broiler. *Makes 6–7 servings.*

Luleh Kabab

Kabâb with Ground Lamb

Luleh Kabâb, or Kufteh Kabâb, as it is sometimes called, is a favorite Persian dish. *Luleh* means rolled, and the Persians call this dish Luleh Kabâb because the meat is rolled into long rolls or around a skewer.

Luleh Kabâb is a very popular luncheon dish in Tehran. If you enter the Tehran Bazaar you may see many merchants sitting in their shops and eating this dish with Nâne Lavâsh and green onions. This dish is not only very delicious and well flavored but is very economical too. It is a popular dish among the rich as well as the poor. It can be quickly prepared and is ideal for summer dinners and picnics.

1 *lb. ground lamb or beef*	1 *tsp. salt*
1 *large onion* (*grated*)	1/2 *tsp. pepper*
1 *egg*	1/4 *tsp. cinnamon*

Put the meat in a bowl. Add grated onions, eggs, and seasoning. Beat the meat with a wooden spoon until the meat seems to turn lighter in color or almost white. Take a handful of the meat mixture and roll it into a roll about the same size as a bread salt stick. Or if you have flat skewers, shape the meat around the skewer 6″ in length and 2″ in diameter. Broil the

 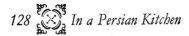

meat on a charcoal broiler for 5–10 minutes or to your own taste. Serve Luleh Kabâb with chelo. It can be served with broiled tomatoes and French bread. *Makes 3–4 servings.*

Kufteh Tabrizi

Tabriz Meat Balls

The word *kufteh*, which literally means "pounded" in Persian, refers to any type of ground meat that has been formed into a meat ball. Persians make a variety of meat balls. They use them in soups, khoreshes, and as a basis for quick meals.

It is said that the best kufteh is made in Azerbaijan and that a Tabriz (capital of Azerbaijan) housewife really has the secret of the best-flavored kufteh. I must say that if this is the case I was fortunate in learning the secret from my mother, who is a native of Tabriz. I remember very well my mother telling me that when she lived in Tabriz, she made a kufteh into which she would put a cooked baby chick. This was cooked in an earthen pot on a very slow fire over hot ashes.

Kufteh Tabrizi is the most famous variety of kufteh prepared in Persia. In this book I am giving you a simplified recipe for this kufteh because the modern American housewife, like the modern Persian housewife, doesn't always have a baby chick available nor does she have the time to cook it over a very slow fire for half a day.

Tabriz Meat Balls

1/2 *cup yellow split peas*	1 *tsp. salt*
3 *cups water*	1/2 *tsp. pepper*
2 *eggs (hard boiled)*	1/2 *tsp. cinnamon*
1 *lb. ground lamb or beef*	1/4 *tsp. nutmeg*
1 *egg*	1/2 *tsp. saffron*
1 *medium onion (grated)*	6 *dried prunes*
1 *tsp. lemon juice*	1/4 *cup water*

Cook the split peas in 3 cups of water for 35–40 minutes or until they can be easily mashed. Peel the boiled eggs and put them aside. Put the meat in a mixing bowl and add 1 raw egg, onions, lemon juice, and seasoning. Strain the water from the cooked peas, mash well, and add to the meat mixture. Mix the meat mixture well. Divide the meat mixture into 2 portions. Make 2 big meat balls and put 1 whole hard-boiled egg and 3 prunes (seeded) in the center of each meat ball. Put the meat balls in a greased pan, add water, and bake in 350° oven for about 40 minutes. *Makes 3–4 servings.*

"It is not right for a guest to stay so long as to incommode his host."
MOHAMMAD

Tas Kabab

Baked Lamb

1 lb. lamb chunks or stewing beef	1/2 tsp. cinnamon
2 large potatoes	1/4 tsp. nutmeg
2 large onions	1/2 tsp. oregano
3 large tomatoes	2 tbsp. butter
1 tsp. salt	1/3 cup water
1/2 tsp. pepper	

Cut the meat in 1″ pieces. Peel and slice the potatoes to 1/8″ thickness. Slice the onions and the tomatoes. Arrange the meat, potatoes, onions, and tomatoes in layers in a greased 9″ casserole. Season each layer well. Top with butter and add water. Bake covered in 325° oven for 30 minutes. Uncover and bake 20 minutes more or until done. *Makes 4 servings.*

Kufteh Gusht

Persian Meat Loaf

I am sure that meat loaf is an international dish, with different spicings in different countries. Kufteh Gusht is a popular dish with the Persian housewife and each housewife adds her own special seasoning to it. This recipe is my mother's, and I think it has just the right seasoning. It is as easy to make as American meat loaf, so do try and surprise your guests with it.

Persian Meat Loaf

1 1/2 *lb. ground lamb or beef*	1/2 *tsp. pepper*
1 *large onion (grated)*	1/4 *tsp. cinnamon*
1/4 *cup finely chopped green onions*	2 *eggs*
1/4 *cup finely chopped parsley*	1/4 *cup tomato paste*
1/4 *cup finely chopped celery leaves*	1 *tbsp. lemon juice*
1 *tsp. salt*	1 *slice white bread*

Put the meat in a large bowl. Add all the above-mentioned ingredients except the bread. Soak the bread in water and squeeze the water and add it to the meat. Mix the meat and the rest well until they are thoroughly mixed. Put it in a baking dish and bake it for 1 hour in a 350° oven. *Makes 4 servings.*

Kotlete Kubideh

Persian Hamburgers

Kotlete Kubideh is my mother's specialty which I have found very handy and economical to make. I have served this on many occasions, especially at picnics, and it has always been very popular. Kotlete Kubideh can be prepared in advance and

 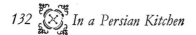

served cold on picnics or for luncheons. It tastes excellent when it is warmed up. If you serve it with chelo just put the kotlet on top of the chelo and warm it in a covered pot. It is ideal for families with children.

1 *lb. ground beef*	1/2 *tsp. pepper*
1 *small onion (grated)*	1/2 *tsp. cinnamon*
1 *egg*	1/4 *tsp. garlic salt*
1–2 *slices bread (soaked in milk)*	1/2 *tsp. oregano*
1 *tsp. salt*	5 *tbsp. shortening*

Put the meat in a bowl. Add the other ingredients and mix well. Make hamburger patties with the meat, round or oval shape. Roll the patties in fine bread crumbs and sauté them in butter or shortening. *Makes 6–8 patties.*

Shami

Tehran Hamburgers

1/2 *lb. stewing beef in* 1" *cubes*	3 *cups water*
1/2 *lb. lamb chunks in* 1" *cubes*	2 *egg yolks*
1 *medium onion (quartered)*	2 *egg whites*
1 *tsp. salt*	1 *tsp. salt*
1/2 *tsp. pepper*	1/4 *tsp. pepper*
1/2 *tsp. cinnamon*	1/4 *tsp. turmerick*
a dash of paprika	1/4 *tsp. saffron (see p. 170)*
1 2/3 *cups water*	6–7 *tsp. shortening*
1 *cup yellow split peas*	

Put the meat in a 2-quart pot. Add onion, seasoning, and

 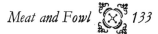

water. Let simmer on a medium fire for about 50 minutes or until tender. Wash and cook yellow split peas in 3 cups of water for about 45 minutes or until they can be easily mashed. Run the cooked meat together with the cooked peas through a food grinder twice. Mash this with a potato masher until the meat and pea mixture is completely mashed. Add egg yolks, the egg whites, and seasoning and mix well with hands. Make hamburger patties and sauté them in shortening. Serve warm or cold. *Makes 15 hamburger patties.*

Abgusht

Lamb Stew

"*Abe Abgushtrâ Ziâd Kon*," is what you might hear the hostess telling her cook when you arrive at someone's house unexpectedly. This phrase, which means "increase the water of Abgusht," is a very popular joke among the Persian housewives. Abgusht is supposed to be a very flexible meal, one which can easily be expanded when unexpected guests arrive for dinner.

Abgusht, which in Persian means "the water of the meat," is one of the most popular dishes in Persia. It is supposedly a poor man's meal, but in fact it is a popular dish with all housewives. It is said that the Azerbaijani housewife knows how to prepare the best Abgusht. In that part of Persia, Abgusht is cooked in a crock for half a day on a very low grill over hot

ashes. The secret of a good Abgusht is the right seasoning and slow cooking.

Basic Abgusht can be varied in several ways. Some housewives prefer to make it watery, serving the broth as a soup and the meat and the rest of the ingredients separately. Others use less water and let it cook until a very thick broth remains. In this book I have given the second method.

Abgusht is a very economical dish. It is prepared with lamb shanks, which are usually cheap and readily available.

2–3 *lamb shanks and/or breast of lamb*	1/2 *tsp. oregano*
1 *large onion* (*sliced*)	1 *tsp. saffron* (*see p. 170*)
1 *tsp. salt*	2 *cups water*
1/2 *tsp. pepper*	1/2 *cup chick peas* (*canned*)
1/2 *tsp. turmerick*	1 *large potato*

Put the meat in a large pot and add the onions, seasoning, and water and let simmer for 1–1 1/2 hours on a very low fire. 20 minutes before serving add chick peas and potato. Add more salt and pepper if necessary. Tomatoes and eggplants may be added when in season. *Makes 4–5 servings.*

Abgushte Gusht Kubideh

Lamb Stew Hash

2–3 *lb. lamb stew or lamb shanks* (*fat trimmed*)	1 *tsp. salt*
1 *cup white beans*	1/2 *tsp. pepper*
2/3 *cup chick peas* (*canned*)	1/2 *tsp. cinnamon*
1 *large onion* (*quartered*)	1/2 *tsp. turmerick*
	6 *cups water*

Put meat in a large pot and add all the above ingredients. Cook for about 3 hours on a very low fire. If stock is left save the stock and use it as a soup. Disjoint the meat from the bones, add the rest of the cooked ingredients to the meat, and mash well with a potato masher. Add more salt and pepper to taste. Serve with dill pickles. *Makes 5–6 servings.*

Abgushte Bademjan

Lamb Stew with Eggplants

1 *large eggplant*	2 *cups water*
4 *tbsp. shortening*	1/2 *tsp. salt*
3–4 *lamb shanks or* 1 1/2 *lb.*	1/4 *tsp. pepper*
shoulder of lamb	1/4 *tsp. cinnamon*
1 *large onion (finely chopped)*	1 *tbsp. lemon juice*
1/4 *cup tomato sauce*	

Cut the unpeeled eggplants lengthwise into 1″ slices. Wash, sprinkle with salt, and let them stand for 20 minutes. Sauté the eggplants in shortening and let stand. Sauté the lamb shanks for a few minutes. Add chopped onions and sauté them for another 5 minutes. Add tomato sauce, water, seasoning, and lemon juice and cover; let cook from 1/2 to 1 hour. About 10 minutes before serving add the sautéed eggplants and let simmer. As a variation try the following: Braise the lamb shanks according to the above recipe. Do not use tomato sauce and replace the eggplants with a couple of quartered apples. Add

to the lamb shanks 15 minutes before serving. Or if you want, add a couple of quartered quinces 25 minutes before serving.

Makes 4 servings.

Abgushte Lubia Germez

Lamb Stew with Kidney Beans

1/3 *cup kidney beans*	1 *bay leaf*
3–4 *lamb shanks*	1 *tsp. oregano*
1 *large onion (finely chopped)*	1/2 *tsp. salt*
2 *tbsp. butter*	1/4 *tsp. pepper*
1/4 *cup tomato sauce*	1/4 *tsp. cinnamon*
2 *cups water*	1 *tbsp. lemon juice*

Wash the kidney beans well. Soak them overnight in enough water to cover. Melt the butter in a pot. Sauté the lamb shanks for several minutes. Add chopped onions and sauté them for another 5 minutes. Add tomato sauce, water, seasoning, lemon juice, and the beans. Cover and let simmer on a very low fire for 1 hour or until the meat is tender. It is excellent eaten with dill pickles.

Makes 3 servings.

"God loveth those who are content."
MOHAMMAD

Khorake Golveh

Sautéed Lamb Kidneys

2 tbsp. butter	6 lamb kidneys
1 large onion (finely chopped)	salt and pepper to taste
1 tbsp. tomato sauce	3 tbsp. shortening

Melt butter in a skillet and sauté the onions for a few minutes. Add tomato sauce and sauté for a few more minutes. Wash and clean the lamb kidneys and cut them up into 4 pieces. Add them to the sautéed onions and sauté them for a few minutes more. Add seasoning, cover, and let simmer on a very low fire. Sauté the potatoes and add them to the kidneys. Let cook for 5 minutes more. *Makes 2–3 servings.*

Jujeh Kabab

Broiled Chicken

2 1/3–3 lb. fryer (cut up)	1 tbsp. oregano
8 tbsp. lemon juice	1/2 tsp. paprika
1/2 cup water	1 tsp. poultry seasoning
1 1/2 tsp. salt	4 tbsp. melted butter
1/2 tsp. pepper	

Wash and pare the chicken for marinating. Marinate the chicken in lemon juice and water about 3 hours. When ready to broil, season it well and brush it with butter. It is best to broil this chicken on the charcoal broiler, however, an oven broiler can be used. Brush the chicken with butter while broiling. Serve the broiled chicken with chelo.

Makes 3–4 servings.

Kufteh Sabzi

Vegetable Meat Balls

2 *tbsp. rice*	1/2 *tsp. pepper*
3 *tbsp. yellow split peas*	1/4 *tsp. cinnamon*
3 *cups water*	3 *tbsp. butter*
1 *lb. ground lamb or beef*	1 *large onion (finely chopped)*
1 *cup green onions (finely chopped)*	3 *tbsp. tomato sauce*
2 *cups parsley (finely chopped)*	1 1/2 *cups water*
1 *egg*	2 *tbsp. lemon juice*
1 *tsp. salt*	

Cook rice and split peas in 3 cups of water for 30 minutes or until tender. Put the meat in a mixing bowl and add green onions, parsley, egg, and seasoning. Strain the water from the cooked peas and rice and add to the meat mixture. Mix well. Make medium-size meat balls and put them aside. Melt butter in a skillet, add the onions and tomato sauce, and sauté the onions until they are light brown. Add 1 1/2 cups of water and lemon juice. Let simmer for 10 minutes. Add meat balls to this sauce, cover, and let simmer for 1/2 hour. Baste the meat balls with the sauce when they are half cooked. This makes 20 medium-size or 7 to 8 large meat balls. *Makes 4–5 servings.*

Khorake Bademjan

Eggplant Casserole with Meat

1 *large eggplant*	1/2 *tsp. pepper*
1/2 *cup shortening*	1/2 *tsp. nutmeg*
1 *large onion (sliced)*	1/2 *tsp. cinnamon*
1 *lb. ground beef*	2 *large tomatoes (sliced)*
2 *cloves garlic (chopped)*	*a dash of paprika*
2 *tsp. salt*	

Cut the eggplants in half (lengthwise), then slice them crosswise in 1/2″ slices. Wash and salt the eggplants. Leave them for 20 minutes. Wash the salt off the eggplants and dry them with a paper towel. Melt shortening in a skillet and sauté the eggplants until golden brown. (As you fry the eggplants put them on a paper towel to absorb the grease.) Sauté the onions in the same skillet until golden brown. Remove them from the pan and put them aside. Sauté the meat until done. Remove the meat and season it well. Grease a pie pan or a casserole. Put in a layer of eggplants, some garlic, meat, tomatoes, and the rest of the

eggplants. Top it with onions. Add a dash of paprika. Bake in
a 300° oven for 20 minutes. Serve it topped with yogurt.
Makes 4–5 servings.

Kababe Morg

Roasted Chicken

2 1/2–3 *lb. roasting chicken or*
  fryer
1 *large onion (finely chopped)*
3 *tbsp. butter*
12 *apricots (chopped)*
6 *prunes (chopped)*
1 *large apple (diced)*
1/4 *cup raisins*

1/4 *cup currants*
1/2 *tsp. salt*
1/4 *tsp. pepper*
1/4 *tsp. cinnamon*
1 *tsp. tarragon*
1/2 *tsp. thyme*
1 1/2 *tsp. saffron (see p. 170)*

Wash and prepare the chicken for roasting. Sauté the
chopped onions in the butter for 5 minutes. Add the dried fruit
and sauté for 5 minutes. Remove, add seasoning, and let cool
for a few minutes. Stuff the chicken with this mixture and roast
for 1 1/2 hours in 350° oven. Serve with chelo. When serving
with chelo, mix the stuffing with the rice. *Makes 3–4 servings.*

"Patience is one-half of religious duty."
ARAB WISDOM

Meat and Fowl 141

Desserts

Since the Persians serve rice as a main dish and since most of the sauces served with it are very filling, the Persian house-wife tries to serve light desserts. If you ever eat at a Persian home, you will be served fresh fruits, when they are in season, or dried fruit compote in winter.

Persians are very fond of fruit. When fruits are in season, they will eat them on any possible occasion. A Persian house-wife will serve fruit at lunch, tea, or dinner. Very often she will serve a bowl of cold fresh fruits: peaches, cherries, strawberries, grapes, melons, oranges, and cucumbers. (In Persia are grown very delicious, delicate cucumbers which are served as a fruit.) When fruit is served after dinner or at tea time, it is customary for the hostess to peel the fruit and pass it to the guests.

However, on special feast days such as Aide Noruz, the Persian New Year, or at weddings and other special occasions, the Persians use their imagination to create exotic desserts such as Bâglavâ, Halvâ, and many other complicated cookies and cakes. In this book I am going to give you a few of the recipes that are easy to follow.

Bâglavâ

Baklava

When I think of Bâglavâ, I think of Aide Noruz, the
Persian New Year, celebrated on the 21st day of March, or the
first day of spring. For this holiday, every Persian housewife
makes her favorite recipe of Bâglavâ. My mother would begin
preparing for Aide Noruz weeks in advance. I can remember
my mother's friends and relatives gathering in our house several
weeks before the Noruz and helping her prepare exotic sweets,
just as American women help their families prepare Christmas
delicacies. My mother knew that if she did not take great pains
with her specialties she would not only disappoint her family
but also her friends, who would make special trips to our house
just to eat her famous Bâglavâ.

The preparation of Bâglavâ and a few other specialties by
my mother such as Nune Shekari (Sugar Cookies) and Bâdâm
Choragi (Almond Cookies) was like a ritual out of story books.
Two or three weeks before Noruz, several women would gather
in one of our large rooms carpeted with an intricately designed
Persian rug. They would sit around a tablecloth, spread on the
floor, upon which stood a large, round wooden board about
two feet high, like a low table. Near the wooden board lay a

rolling pin, not like the kind used in America, but a long thin stick the size and shape of a cane. Every woman had a hand in this preparation. One would blanch the almonds, another would chop them. A third would break the conically shaped sugar loaves, the usual form in which sugar is sold in Persia. She would pound the sugar in a mortar until it became powdered. Another woman would mix the chopped almonds, sugar, cardamom, and other ingredients. The preparation of the dough and the rolling part was my mother's task. She never allowed anyone else to do this, for the secret of good Bâglavâ lies in the thinness of the dough.

None of the Persian homes that I knew was adequately equipped for baking. If a Persian housewife wanted to bake anything more than ordinary cakes or cookies, she was obliged to take her dough to a regular baker and leave whatever she intended to bake with the baker, or stay there until her dough was baked. Since we used to make not just 40 or 50 pieces of Bâglavâ, but sometimes 150 or more, my mother was always obliged to take her Bâglavâ to a nearby bakery. Of course, she could send it over by servants and trust the baker to time it correctly, but she never did that. She never trusted anyone but herself with this delicate task. I do not think I ever missed going with Mother to the bakery with the Bâglavâ. Perhaps I accompanied her because I was fascinated with this whole ceremony and wanted to take part in the preparation or perhaps it was because I knew that when the Bâglavâ was finished baking Mother would let me have a piece or two.

In my opinion Bâglavâ is the queen of all pastries, if properly prepared. Like any other delicate pastry you should know just how much and what to use in order to get the exotic flavor.

 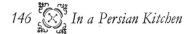

I just hope I have not scared you after telling you about the ritual my mother used to go through. Bâglavâ is actually a very easy pastry to make. In the first place, the hard part of making Bâglavâ, the pastry, can be bought ready made. And in the second place, with the modern gas or electric range, you don't need to go to the nearest bakery to have your Bâglavâ baked. So let us follow my mother's recipe, for this is one recipe that you will not find anywhere else. Some of you, I am sure, have tasted Bâglavâ in a Greek or Armenian restaurant, but believe me, this recipe is something special. As for pastry and rose water, you can buy them in any Greek or Armenian or Syrian store in your town.

Baklava

4 *cups blanched chopped almonds*	1 *lb. sweet butter* (*melted*)
2 *cups sugar* (*granulated*)	2 *cups granulated sugar*
1/2 *tbsp. cardamom*	1 *cup water*
1 *lb. ready Baklava pastry* (*see p. 169*)	2 *tbsp. rose water* (*see p. 170*)

Blanch the almonds. Let them dry. Chop them very finely in the nut chopper. Put the chopped almonds in a bowl, add sugar and cardamom, and mix well. Grease a 13 × 9 × 2″ pan. Put 3 layers of pastry in the pan and brush with butter after each layer. (This pastry should be handled with care so that it will not become dry.) Spread the almond mixture evenly on top of each layer. Cover it with a layer of pastry. Repeat this, and brush with butter after each layer. Put 2 layers of pastry on the top and brush them with butter. Cut this pastry in diamond shapes. Pour the melted butter over it evenly. Bake it in a 350° oven for 35–40 minutes or until it is golden color.

Boil the sugar with water for 20–25 minutes on a medium

fire. Add rose water to this syrup and let stay for a while. When Bâglavâ is ready pour the sugar syrup over the Bâglavâ and let it cool. If rose water can't be obtained, substitute it with one tablespoon of lemon juice and a couple of cinnamon sticks boiled with sugar and water.

Sekanjabin

Sweet-and-Sour Syrup

Sekanjabin is a syrupy substance which is used by the Persians in summer. A Persian housewife uses Sekanjabin for many purposes. She uses it as a base for a cool drink. 3 to 4 tablespoons of Sekanjabin with a couple of ice cubes and plain water or soda makes a very delicious and refreshing drink. Sekanjabin can also be used as a dessert. Dip romaine lettuce in a bowl of Sekanjabin and eat it; you will find a very delightful and light dessert. You might also try the combination of diced cucumbers, Sekanjabin, and corn flakes.

2 *cups water*	1 1/2 *cups vinegar*
6 *cups sugar*	*couple stalks mint*

Put the water in a pan, add sugar, and let it boil on a medium fire until the sugar is dissolved. Add vinegar and boil for 15 or 20 minutes more. Remove from the fire, add mint, and let

it cool. The consistency of Sekanjabin should be like syrup. Serve with romaine lettuce.

Compote Miveh Tazeh

Fresh Fruit Compote

1 *cup sugar*	3 *plums*
4 *cups water*	1 *cup strawberries*
2 *tart apples*	2 *tbsp. lemon juice*
2 *peaches*	2–3 *sticks cinnamon*

Put 1 cup of sugar in a pot. Add water and let cook until it comes to the boiling point. Wash, pare, quarter, core, and slice apples and peaches in 1/4″ thicknesses. Wash and clean the plums and strawberries. Put the fruit in the prepared syrup. Add lemon juice and spices. Let simmer on a medium fire for about 10 minutes or until done. Store in refrigerator to cool. Serve cold or, if desired, add whipped cream. The fruits in this compote may vary. You can use any combination of fruits such as cherries, apricots, pears, etc. *Makes 6–7 servings.*

"Patience is one of the gifts of heaven."
ARAB WISDOM

Halva

Sweet Dessert

1 *cup butter or shortening*
2 *cups flour (sifted)*
1 1/2 *cups sugar*

1 *cup water*
1 1/2 *tbsp. saffron (see p. 170)*

Boil the sugar in 1 cup of water. Melt butter in a deep skillet. Add flour gradually, stirring constantly. Stir the flour and butter mixture on a medium fire until it is light caramel color. Remove from fire. Add 1/2 cup of the melted sugar and stir vigorously. Add the rest of the melted sugar and saffron and stir well. When ready Halvâ should look like peanut butter. Halvâ can be used as a dessert or it can be eaten like peanut butter on bread.

Nane Shirini

Persian Cookies

2 *cups flour*
1 *tsp. baking powder*
1 *cup shortening*
1 *cup granulated sugar*

2 *egg yolks*
1 *tsp. vanilla*
1 *tsp. almond extract*
1 *tsp. lemon extract*

Sift together 2 cups of flour and 1 teaspoon of baking powder.

Cream thoroughly 1 cup shortening and 1 cup granulated sugar. Blend in 2 egg yolks, vanilla, almond extract, and lemon extract. Mix well. Add gradually the dry ingredients and mix until dough is well blended. Roll dough into round balls with hands, using about 1 level teaspoon of dough for each ball. Place on ungreased baking sheet and flatten slightly with a spoon. Bake in a slow oven of 235° for 20 minutes. *Makes 30–40 cookies.*

Compote Koshkbar

Dried Fruit Compote

Compote Khoshkbâr is a very popular winter dessert. In the winter, when fresh fruit is very scarce in Persia, the Persian housewife makes use of the very excellent dried fruits for which Persia is famous and prepares a delicious compote dessert for her family.

5 *cups water*	1 *cup dried apples*
1 *cup sugar*	1/2 *cup dried apricots*
12 *prunes (dried)*	1–2 *tbsp. rose water (see p. 170)*

Boil water with sugar for 10 minutes or until the sugar is melted. Wash prunes and boil them in this syrup for 5 minutes. Add apples and apricots and let simmer on a low fire for approximately 15 minutes. Add rose water and let cool. Serve cold. If desired, serve with cream. *Makes 4–5 servings.*

Pâludeh

Persian Delights

Pâludeh is a typical Persian dessert which is served either as grated or crushed fresh fruit, topped with crushed ice, and flavored with rose water or as a combination of starchy substance and fruit syrup such as cherries or quince, etc., topped with crushed ice. In Persia pâludeh is served like ice cream. One can serve it at any time and it can be ordered at any restaurant.

Pâludeh is a very easy dessert to prepare. In this book I have given the recipe for the "fresh fruit" pâludeh which can be quickly prepared. Do try to serve pâludeh when you have guests and surprise them with this simple and yet very exotic dessert.

Melon Delight

1 *medium cantaloupe or Persian melon*	2 *tbsp. lemon juice*
	1/2 *tsp. salt*
2 *ripe peaches*	2 *tbsp. rose water (see p. 170)*
1/3 *cup sugar*	*crushed ice*

Cut the melon in half and scoop out as many melon balls as you can. Put them in a crockery bowl. Save the melon juice and add it to the melon balls. It is important that you use all

 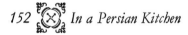

the melon juice. Peel the peaches and slice them thinly. Add this to the melon balls. Add sugar, lemon juice, and salt. Let stand in the frigidaire for a few hours. 1/2 hour before serving, add rose water and put it back in the icebox. Right before serving put the melon mixture in individual serving dishes and top it with very finely crushed ice. *Makes 5–6 servings.*

Apple Delight

4 *medium apples*
2 *tbsp. lemon juice*
5 *tbsp. powdered sugar*

2 *tsp. rose water (see p. 170)*
crushed ice

Peel the apples and grate them. Sprinkle the grated apples with lemon juice. (This process prevents the apples from darkening.) Add sugar and rose water and stir lightly. Let stand in the refrigerator for a few hours. 10 minutes before serving add crushed ice and serve. *Makes 3–4 servings.*

Desere Holu

Peach Dessert

4 *peaches (not very ripe)*
2/3 *cup water*
1/3 *cup sugar*

1 *tsp. rose water (see p. 170) or*
1/2 *tsp. cardamom*

Peel and slice the peaches. Pour water in a small pan, add sugar, and let come to a boiling point. Add peaches and let simmer in this syrup for 5 minutes. Cool. When ready to serve, add either rose water or cardamom. Serve over vanilla ice cream or serve with whipped cream.

If peaches are not in season, canned peaches may be used. Heat peaches in their own syrup and add rose water or sprinkle with cardamom and your favorite liqueur. *Makes 4–5 servings.*

Shir Berenj

Rice Pudding

The Persians make many uses of rice. They use rice in soups, as a main course, and they also make very delicious desserts from it. Shir Bereng, made of rice and milk, is a very delicious dessert which is more or less like the American rice pudding. The touch of rose water or cardamom, I think, makes it a quite different and very refreshing dessert.

1/4 *cup rice*	1 *tsp. rose water (see p. 170) or cardamom*
1 *cup water*	*powder*
3 *cups milk*	1 1/2 *tbsp. sugar*
1/4 *tsp. salt*	*cinnamon*

Wash rice well. Boil rice in 2 cups of water for about 25 minutes or until the water is almost absorbed. Add milk, salt,

 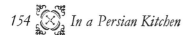

rose water, and sugar and let boil on a medium fire for about 25 minutes or until the milk is absorbed and the rice is done. Pour into small pudding dishes. Decorate with cinnamon and let cool. Store in the icebox until serving time. Serve cold. Add honey or sugar when serving.   *Makes 4–5 servings.*

> *"Riches are not from abundance of worldly goods, but from a contented mind."*
>
> MOHAMMAD

Salads

Salade Sabzi

Vegetable Salad

There is an old Persian saying that it takes four people to prepare salad: a generous man to add the oil, a stingy man to add the vinegar, a wise man to give it the right touch of salt and pepper, and a fool to mix it well.

Persians, like most people, are fond of green salads. When fresh vegetables are in season, they try to eat green salad with every meal. Each housewife, of course, has her own special salad dressing. In this book I shall give you my favorite salad dressing. I have served this many times to my American friends.

1 *head romaine lettuce*	1/2 *cup parsley (chopped)*
1 *cucumber (sliced thin)*	1/4 *cup dill (chopped) or* 1 *tbsp.*
2 *tomatoes (sliced or quartered)*	*dill weed*
1/4 *cup green onions (chopped)*	1/4 *cup mint leaves or* 1 *tsp. dry mint*
3 *radishes (sliced thin)*	*white goat's cheese*

Rub a large wooden bowl with garlic. Wash and dry all the above vegetables. Do not cut the lettuce with knife, handle it by hand. Add all the rest of the vegetables and cheese. Do not make the salad too far in advance. If you must, however, be sure to keep it in the refrigerator. *Makes 5–6 servings.*

Salad Dressing

1/3 *cup olive oil*
3 *tbsp. fresh lemon juice*
1/2 *tsp. salt*
1/4 *tsp. black pepper*

a dash of garlic salt or 1 *clove garlic*
  squeezed
1/2 *tsp. sugar*

Mix all the above-mentioned ingredients and shake well. Just before serving, add to the salad and toss.

"*No father hath given his child any-thing better than good manners.*"

MOHAMMAD

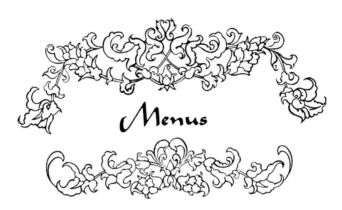

Menus

NEW YEAR'S DINNER
Shâme Aide Noruz

Nâzkhâtun
Eggplant Caviar

Panir va Nâne Lavâsh
Goat's Cheese and Persian bread

Dolmeh Barg
Stuffed Grape Leaves

Mâst
Yogurt

Chelo bâ Khoreshe Fesenjân
Rice with Pomegranate Sauce

Morg Polo
Rice with Chicken

Sâlâde Sabzi
Vegetable Salad

Bâglavâ
Baklava

Châi bâ Limu
Tea with Lemon

Miveh
Fruit in Season

SUMMER LUNCHEON

Kukuye Sib Zamini va Gojeh Farangi
Potato and Tomato Casserole

Nâne Lavâsh
Persian Bread

Salâde Sabzi
Vegetable Salad

Kâhu va Sekanjabin
Romaine Lettuce with Sweet-and-Sour Syrup

Châi
Tea

SUMMER LUNCHEON

Nân va Panir bâ Nanâ va Tarkhun
Bread with Goat's Cheese, Fresh Mint, and Tarragon

Mâst va Khiâr
Yogurt with Cucumbers

Kukuye Sabzi
Vegetable Casserole

Pâludeh Kharbozeh
Melon Delight

Sharbate Sekanjabin
Sweet-and-Sour Syrup

164  *In a Persian Kitchen*

SUMMER DINNER

Dolmeh Sib
Stuffed Apples

Mâst va Khiâr
Yogurt with Cucumbers

Chelo bâ Khoreshe Rivâs
Rice with Rhubarb Sauce

Kharbozeh
Persian Melon

Châi bâ Limu
Tea with Lemon

SUMMER DINNER

Borâni Esfanâj
Spinach Hors d'oeuvre

Soupe Mâst va Khiâr
Cold Yogurt Soup

Chelo Kabâb
Rice with Broiled Lamb

Sâlâde Sabzi
Green Salad

Abdug
Diluted Yogurt with Water

Miveh
Fresh Fruit

WINTER LUNCHEON

Borâni Chogondar
Beet Hors d'oeuvre

Ashe Reshte
Noodle Soup

Adas Polo
Rice with Lentils

Pâludeh Sib
Apple Delight

Châi bâ Limu
Tea with Lemon

WINTER DINNER

Ashe Miveh
Dried Fruit Soup

Khorâke Jujeh
Roast Chicken

Bâgâli Polo
Rice with Lima Beans

Mâst
Yogurt

Halvâ
Sweet Dessert

Châi bâ Limu
Tea with Lemon

 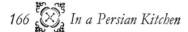

WINTER DINNER

Ashe Mâst
Hot Yogurt Soup

Kufteh Tabrizi
Tabriz Meat Balls

Chelo Khoreshe Geimeh
Rice with Meat and Pea Sauce

Compote Miveh Khoshk
Dried Fruit Compote

Châi bâ Limu
Tea with Lemon

Appendix

Persian Uses and Descriptions of Herbs, Spices, and Unusual Ingredients

ALLSPICE: A spice used with meats, sauces, stuffings, etc.

BAY LEAVES: May be used in soups, stews, poultry, etc.

BAKLAVA PASTRY: Very thin layers of dough which may be purchased in Greek or Armenian bakeries and groceries.

CARDAMOM SEEDS AND POWDER: Used in baking pastry or desserts. May be purchased in large groceries or specialty stores.

CINNAMON STICKS AND POWDER: A spice often used in seasoning meats and poultry and in baking pastry and in desserts.

CURRY POWDER: Used to season meats, eggs, poultry, and sauces made with yogurt.

DILL: The Persians use a great deal of fresh dill with rice, meat, salads, soups, and yogurt. Dill weed may be substituted when fresh dill isn't available. Fresh dill may be purchased in Greek, Armenian, or Italian groceries.

GARLIC: Used for meats, salads, soups, and some sauces.

GOAT'S CHEESE: White cheese, which in Persian is called *panir*. Used in salads or appetizers with fresh mint or tarragon. May be purchased in Greek or Armenian stores under the name *fetâ*.

GRAPE LEAVES: Grape leaves are used for Dolmeh, or stuffed grape leaves. Preserved grape leaves may be purchased in Greek or Armenian stores.

MINT: Mint, fresh or dry, is much used by the Persians. Fresh mint is used in drinks and salads, and dry mint in combination with cinnamon and black pepper is used in seasoning soups, sauces, etc.

NUTMEG: May be used in seasoning lamb, meats, sauces, vegetables, and pastries.

OREGANO: May be used in seasoning lamb, meats, stews, and salads.

PAPRIKA: Used for soups, meats, salads, salad dressings, and garnishings.

POMEGRANATE SYRUP: Used in preparing khoreshes and sauces. May be purchased in Greek or Armenian stores.

POULTRY SEASONING: Used in seasoning game and poultry.

RICE: For Persian polo or chelo long-grain white rice should be used. Brands such as "North Carolina" long grain or "Show Boat" give very good results.

ROSE WATER: Rose water is used in desserts, pastries, and drinks. It can be purchased in Greek or Armenian groceries.

SAFFRON: Often used in seasoning rice, lamb, sauces, and pastry. Saffron may be purchased in any large grocery store or at Greek or Armenian stores. If you use "Spice Island" powdered saffron, follow the directions given, and for seasoning Persian dishes use a tablespoon or two of the saffron which has been dissolved in water according to the directions.

SUMAC: Sumac is a spice which looks like chili powder and has a somewhat sour taste. It is used with meats, especially broiled meats such as kabâb or steaks. May be purchased in Armenian or Greek groceries.

TARRAGON: In Persia fresh tarragon is used extensively with meats, salads, cheese, etc. Since fresh tarragon is scarce in America, dry tarragon can be substituted and used in seasoning, stuffings, lamb, salads, and meats.

THYME: Used for seasoning game, poultry, lamb, stuffing, etc.

TURMERICK: Widely used in Persia for rice, meats, stews, and in baking.

Index

Index 173